PRINCETON STUDIES IN INTERNATIONAL FINANCE
No. 74, December 1992

SHOULD THE MAASTRICHT TREATY BE SAVED?

BARRY EICHENGREEN

INTERNATIONAL FINANCE SECTION
DEPARTMENT OF ECONOMICS
PRINCETON UNIVERSITY
PRINCETON, NEW JERSEY

Library of Congress Cataloging-in-Publication Data

Eichengreen, Barry J.
Should the Maastricht Treaty be saved? / Barry Eichengreen.
p. cm.—(Princeton studies in international finance, ISSN 0081-8070 ; no. 74)
Includes bibliographical references.
ISBN 0-88165-246-6 (pbk.) : $9.00
1. Monetary unions—European Economic Community countries. 2. Monetary policy—European Economic Community countries. I. Title. II. Series.
HG930.5.E43 1992
332.4'566'094—dc20 92-46576
CIP

Printed in the United States of America by Princeton University Press at Princeton, New Jersey

International Standard Serial Number: 0081-8070
International Standard Book Number: 0-88165-246-6
Library of Congress Catalog Card Number: 92-46576

CONTENTS

FIGURES

TABLES

1 INTRODUCTION

The successful negotiation by government leaders of the Maastricht Treaty in December 1991 seemed to shift the process of European Economic and Monetary Union (EMU) into high gear. Subsequent events, however, have eliminated the sense of inevitability with which post-Maastricht observers regarded the prospects for EMU. The treaty's defeat in the Danish referendum first exposed the extent of public resistance, implying that at least a cosmetic revision of the treaty would be necessary for it to gain unanimous ratification by European Community (EC) member countries. The slim margin of victory in the subsequent French referendum underscored the point. Perhaps most important, the exchange-market crisis in the days leading up to the French vote on September 20 revealed the market's skepticism that European governments were adequately committed to their pegged exchange rates and, by implication, its doubts about the viability of the Maastricht blueprint for EMU.

A debate that had once seem closed now seems certain to be reopened. The immediate question is whether the Maastricht Treaty should be saved. But the underlying issue—the desirability of European monetary unification—is also back on the table.

The goal of this paper is to bring up to date the discussion of EMU and the Maastricht Treaty. The study reviews what is known about the costs and benefits of monetary unification, examines the institutional concomitants of a successful monetary union, and analyzes specific provisions of the Maastricht Treaty.

Two likely consequences of post-Maastricht developments are increased pressure for subsidiarity and a greater likelihood of multispeed EMU.

Financial support for this research was provided by the Center for German and European Studies of the University of California at Berkeley. I thank Morris Goldstein, Christopher Pissarides, and Geoffrey Woglom for data, Luisa Lambertini and Graham Schindler for research assistance, and Tamim Bayoumi for permission to draw on some of our joint work. Helpful comments were provided by Paul De Grauwe, Jacques Melitz, Richard Portes, and Jürgen von Hagen. Remaining errors are of course my own. Portions of this paper were written during visits to the International Monetary Fund and the Board of Governors of the Federal Reserve System, the hospitality of which is gratefully acknowledged. The views expressed here are not necessarily those of any of the above-mentioned individuals or organizations.

The central conclusion of this paper is that both trends may prove problematic. The increased likelihood that EMU will start with the participation of only a subset of EC members highlights the inadequacies of the Maastricht Treaty's provisions governing entry. Moreover, although a smoothly functioning monetary union requires more centralization of economic functions than is provided for under the treaty, the skepticism shown by Danish and French voters with regard to the idea of a federal Europe is bound to lead to less centralization, not more.

The analysis proceeds in six parts. Chapter 2 reviews the potential benefits of monetary unification, including lower transactions costs, greater price stability, and deeper market integration. The central question is whether monetary union is essential to achieve these goals or whether they can be attained through less radical measures, namely, firmly fixed exchange rates between existing currencies. I conclude that, although the advantages of monetary union over fixed exchange rates between national currencies are less transparent than suggested by many advocates of EMU, truly fixing exchange rates between distinct currencies remains infeasible in the present economic and political setting. As a consequence, monetary union conveys benefits not available under the other practical alternatives.

Chapter 3 considers the other side of the coin, the costs of monetary union. The magnitude of those costs depends on the incidence of shocks and on the usefulness of the exchange rate as an instrument for adjusting to them. Alternatives to the exchange rate as an adjustment mechanism include wage and price changes, interregional migration, interregional capital flows, and interregional fiscal transfers. I consider each mechanism in turn.

Chapter 4 highlights fiscal issues. I suggest that fiscal federalism, which is not provided for in the Maastricht Treaty, has a role to play in monetary union, but that fiscal restraints of the sort adopted at Maastricht do not.

Chapter 5 turns to the design of the European Central Bank (ECB). Key issues in its design are to insure its independence from political pressure and to determine whether or not it should assume responsibility for prudential supervision. I identify some limitations in the provisions of the treaty with regard to guaranteeing the independence necessary for price stability, and I argue that the decision at Maastricht to relieve the ECB of responsibility for prudential supervision may be a serious mistake.[1]

Chapter 6 considers the transition: how Europe should move from its present system of pegged but adjustable exchange rates to a single currency and a European central bank. I raise questions about the appropriateness of the convergence criteria adopted at Maastricht for determining which countries will qualify for participation in EMU.

Chapter 7 turns from a focus on European affairs to EMU's impact on the rest of the world. Conventional wisdom has it that the creation of a single European currency will increase the global demand for the ECU and reduce the demand for dollars. I suggest that, even if EMU stimulates the demand for ECUs and reduces the demand for dollars, the net effect is likely to be small, partly because historical and institutional factors inhibit shifts among currencies and partly because the desire for diversified portfolios on the part of Europeans will stimulate the demand for non-European currencies.

Chapter 7 also considers the prospects for international policy coordination following EMU. Although the reduction in the number of players in the European monetary arena from twelve to one would attenuate some of the problems plaguing efforts to coordinate policies among large numbers of participants, I conclude that other aspects of the EMU process do not bode well for more systematic policy coordination between Europe, the United States, and Japan.

[1] The Statute of the ECB and of the European System of Central Banks (ESCB) is contained in Title VI of the Amendments to the European Economic Community (EEC) Treaty as agreed in the European Council of Maastricht on December 10, 1991 (see Conference of the Representatives of the Governments of the Member States, 1991).

2 BENEFITS OF MONETARY UNIFICATION

The benefits of monetary unification fall under three headings: the reduction in transactions costs associated with the elimination of national currencies, the increased credibility of the participating governments' commitment to price stability, and the greater efficiency of resource allocation through the elimination of exchange-rate-related uncertainty.

Lower Transactions Costs

Tourists (and professors) changing money at European airports cannot help but be impressed by the transactions costs associated with the existence of national currencies. These commissions, averaging several percent, will be eliminated by the creation of a single currency. The tourist's impression, however, overstates the magnitude of the potential savings, for commissions on wholesale transactions for corporations and others are considerably smaller than those on retail exchanges.

Evidence about the magnitude of these savings is scanty. The European Commission (1990) conjectures that currency conversion costs an average of 2.5 percent for travelers but is as little as 0.05 percent for retail transactions in excess of $5 million. The commission contends that conversion costs absorb some 0.1 percent of gross domestic product (GDP) for larger member states whose currencies are used extensively for international payments but rise to as much as 1 percent of GDP for the Community's small, open, less-developed economies. They are said to average 0.4 percent of GDP for the EC as a whole.

Fourth-tenths of a percentage point of GDP seems like a small return on a process riddled with uncertainties and pitfalls. Even if one adds the benefits of simplified accounting and cash-management procedures, the reduction in transactions costs still seems small. Many harbor the suspicion that there are larger gains to be reaped—that the bounded rationality of consumers and producers means that creating a Community-wide unit of account will, by reducing the costs of processing information, enhance the efficiency of resource allocation. I return to these arguments below.

Enhancing Price Stability

Inflation rates declined and converged throughout Europe in the 1980s. A popular presumption is that the European Monetary System (EMS) was responsible. More inflation-prone countries were forced to reduce their inflation rates to German levels by pegging their currencies to the deutsche mark. By doing so, they effectively delegated their monetary policies to the Bundesbank, an institution with a credible anti-inflationary reputation.

But EMS parities are not written in stone, and market participants are aware that countries retain the option to realign, as Frankel and Phillips (1991) show. Hence, the anti-inflationary credibility lent by the EMS remains incomplete. Inflation-prone countries can continue to pursue policies more expansionary than those of Germany and to devalue once their real exchange rates appreciate to unsustainable levels. Only monetary unification, which eliminates this option by abolishing exchange rates, ensures that inflation rates in other European countries will decline permanently to German levels.

A problem with this argument, as Collins (1988) notes, is that EMS membership may not in fact have contributed to the decline of European inflation rates in the 1980s. Inflation declined in EMS and non-EMS countries alike, as Figure 1 shows. After controlling for other determinants of inflation, Collins finds that EMS membership had no residual impact on a country's inflation performance through 1985.[2] Changing attitudes toward inflation rather than EMS membership per se appear to account for the decline in inflation (Collins and Giavazzi, 1993). In other words, the enhanced price stability produced by this public support made exchange-rate stability possible, not the other way around.

Collins' conclusion derived from regressions using data from a cross section of some two dozen EMS and non-EMS countries for the period from 1971 to 1985. She regressed inflation on lagged money growth, lagged GDP growth, and changes in inflation over preceding years. Dummy variables represented participation in the EMS and in its predecessor, the Snake. When a dummy variable for the 1979-1985 subperiod was included, EMS membership during that subperiod was seen to have no discernible impact on a country's inflation performance.

Collins' data end in 1985, which may predate the period in which the EMS gained full credibility and its anti-inflationary effects became evident. As Figure 1 shows, inflation declined less rapidly in EMS countries in the first half of the 1980s but more rapidly thereafter. The first three columns of Table 1 therefore update Collins' analysis to 1990. When EMS status between 1986 and 1990 is added to her basic

[2] Grilli, Masciandaro, and Tabellini (1991) also find no impact of EMS membership on inflation after controlling for its other determinants.

FIGURE 1

CPI INFLATION IN EMS AND NON-EMS COUNTRIES

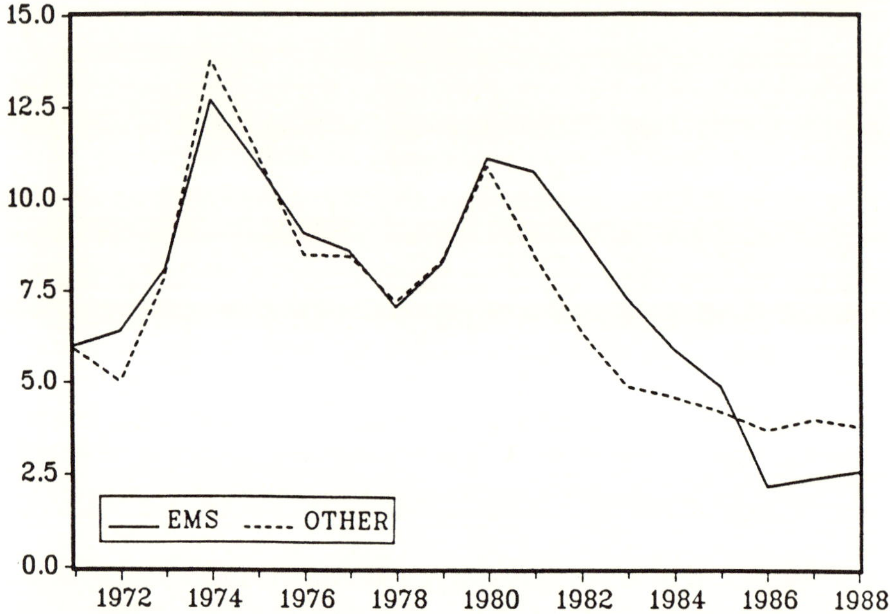

SOURCE: De Grauwe, 1992, p. 123.

specification without also adding a dummy variable for those years, membership appears to have been associated with significantly lower inflation. But, once the 1986-1990 dummy is added, the EMS effect, while still negative, loses its significance.

An objection to this procedure is that the same EMS dummy is used for Germany as for countries pegging to the deutsche mark. Because there is no reason to think that EMS membership reduced German inflation, Germany's inclusion could bias the results against the finding of a significant anti-inflationary effect. Columns four through six of Table 1 therefore report the results of estimating the same equations with Germany omitted from the sample. Its removal does not weaken the basic result.

This analysis, which reinforces Collins' finding, suggests that changing attitudes toward inflation were conducive to exchange-rate stability and the emergence of the EMS, not that the EMS played a causal role in bringing down European inflation. Countries like Austria, which did not participate formally in the EMS but nonetheless shadowed the deutsche

TABLE 1

INFLATION AND THE EMS

(dependent variable is annualized rate of inflation)

	(1)	(2)	(3)	(4)	(5)	(6)
Constant	7.73	8.09	8.44	8.31	8.55	8.10
	(15.66)	(15.45)	(12.54)	(15.67)	(12.66)	(16.01)
M1	0.39	0.38	0.38	0.39	0.38	0.38
	(10.80)	(10.60)	(10.57)	(10.38)	(10.28)	(10.46)
GDP	-0.51	-0.51	-0.51	0.52	-0.53	-0.52
	(-5.05)	(-5.17)	(-5.13)	(-5.17)	(-5.20)	(-5.11)
$(\Pi_t - \Pi_{t-1})$[a]	0.59	0.59	0.59	0.58	0.58	0.59
	(8.63)	(8.61)	(8.63)	(8.52)	(8.47)	(8.55)
EMS (1974-78)	—	—	-0.66	—	0.26	—
	—	—	(-0.74)	—	(0.28)	—
EMS (1986-90)	—	-1.38	-1.25	-0.92	-0.68	—
	—	(-2.01)	(-1.65)	(-1.32)	(-0.86)	—
1986-85	-1.32	-1.35	-1.35	-0.96	-0.97	-0.94
	(-1.37)	(-1.41)	(-1.41)	(-0.94)	(-0.95)	(-0.92)
1986-90	—	—	-0.48	—	-0.49	—
	—	—	(-.72)	—	(-0.73)	—
N	344	344	344	327	327	327
R-squared	0.49	0.49	0.50	0.50	0.50	0.49
F-statistic	64.57	54.96	41.16	52.61	39.45	62.64

SOURCE: Collins, 1988, and author's calculations.

NOTE: *t*-statistics are in parentheses.

[a] Lagging this variable did not generally alter the regression results.

mark, and other countries that did not peg to the EMS but instead pursued independent exchange-rate policies, did as well on average in fighting inflation as Germany's EMS partners. The implication is that solidifying the EMS by continuing down the path toward monetary unification is neither necessary nor sufficient for buttressing price stability.

Promoting Market Integration

Another potential benefit of EMU, in addition to reducing transactions costs and enhancing price stability, is its contribution to market integration. Because eliminating exchange-rate uncertainty encourages international trade, the establishment of a single currency will promote trade among EC countries. Yet, the vast majority of studies of exchange-rate uncertainty and trade (surveyed by IMF, 1983) find little evidence of an important link. Sapir and Sekket (1989), focusing on EC countries, find only a small effect. This is not surprising, as traders can use currency diversification and forward markets to lessen the risks attendant on exchange-rate changes.

Another variant of the argument, emphasized by McKinnon (1963), is that uncertainty in general, and exchange-rate uncertainty in particular, discourage investment. But there exists little empirical support for the view that exchange-rate uncertainty depresses the level of capital formation. Kenen (1979) estimated an investment equation for sixteen industrial countries, including among his independent variables the month-to-month volatility of exchange rates. Although negative, the coefficient on exchange-rate variability was almost never statistically distinguishable from zero.

Rather than affecting the level of investment, exchange-rate uncertainty may influence who invests where. Although an extensive literature examines the link between exchange-rate variability and foreign investment, few of the relevant studies consider the EC in particular. One exception is Morsink and Molle (1991), who offer some relatively weak evidence that exchange-rate uncertainty depresses direct foreign investment within the EC. This is plausible insofar as direct investments have long half-lives and forward contracts of such duration do not exist. Yet, there are other ways to minimize the risks created by exchange-rate variability, notably portfolio diversification. Cushman (1988) reports evidence of a positive association between exchange-rate variability and foreign investment, which he explains by linking exchange-rate uncertainty to the desire to diversify direct-investment portfolios across currencies. The marginal significance of Morsink's and Molle's results may reflect the presence of this offsetting effect.

A more general form of the argument (Commission, 1990) is that monetary unification is a necessary prerequisite for the rest of the Single Market (or 1992) Program. The logic runs as follows. The EMS of the 1980s was a hybrid of fixed and flexible exchange rates. Extended periods of exchange-rate stability delivered many of the benefits of fixed rates. Periodic realignments redressed serious problems of competitiveness. Interludes of exchange-rate stability punctuated by occasional realignments were possible, however, only because capital controls protected the central banks' reserves against speculative attacks provoked by anticipations of a realignment. Thus sheltered, countries could pursue independent monetary policies initially and realign later. But capital controls were incompatible with the rest of the 1992 Program. It was hardly feasible to restrict the freedom of Frenchmen to open bank accounts in Germany, for example, while eliminating all controls on intra-EC movements of portfolio capital and direct foreign investment, not to mention labor and commodities. Hence, controls were a casualty of the 1992 Program, and monetary unification followed inevitably.

There are two problems with the above argument. First, it is far from clear that monetary unification is the only alternative left by the removal of capital controls. Another option, of course, is to revert to floating exchange rates. But floating within Europe has been deemed incompatible with the rest of the 1992 Program.[3] It is perplexing that there has been so little discussion of this option; free-trade negotiations between the United States, Canada, and Mexico have proceeded, after all, without any discussion of currency unification or even of exchange-rate stabilization.[4] It is not obvious that floating exchange rates between the North American Free Trade Agreement (NAFTA) partners represent a significant barrier to regional integration.

Second, it is not clear that the removal of capital controls actually threatens the viability of fixed rates. As Gros and Thygesen (1992) note, capital controls have always been permeable. Moreover, there exist counterexamples to the proposition: the exchange rate between the Belgian and Luxembourg francs, for instance, has been fixed for more than fifty years, a stability in which capital controls have played no role. Retailers and banks in Luxembourg accept Belgian francs at the same rate as local currency because the probability of exchange-rate changes is regarded as minimal. Why could not the EC, like Luxembourg, reap the benefits of a common currency simply by fixing the exchange rates between its twelve national currencies?

The standard answer is that Luxembourg's situation is unique in that it possesses neither a central bank nor monetary independence.[5] A

[3] Giovannini (1992) provides a forceful expression of the prevailing European position, suggesting that floating rates disrupt the EC's Common Agricultural Policy (CAP), which supports the domestic-currency prices of agricultural commodities in member countries. With domestic-currency prices fixed, exchange-rate changes within the Community create an incentive to ship these commodities from one member country to another, disrupting efforts to maintain an "orderly market." The irony of this explanation is that opposition to a return to floating in Europe is grounded, not in the desire to liberalize markets, but in an effort to support restrictions on freedom of agricultural production and trade.

[4] See, however, McLeod and Welch (1991a and b) and Bayoumi and Eichengreen (1993b).

[5] The Luxembourg Monetary Institute is more like a currency board. It is bound by a treaty with Belgium and can only issue a certain amount of currency. But, even for Luxembourg, it is conceivable that a central bank and an independent monetary policy might be established in the future. Reflecting this fact, foreign-exchange cover for Luxembourg francs begins to cost positive amounts as one moves from spot transactions free of transactions costs to those with longer maturities (Gros and Thygesen, 1992, p. 231).

national central bank, the argument runs, cannot commit itself completely to defending the exchange rate, no matter how strongly it asserts its intention to do so. If it continues to control monetary policy, it retains the option of reneging on that commitment. Hence, declarations that it is committed to the maintenance of the existing exchange rate will never be fully credible, and speculative runs will be inevitable. The exchange-rate crisis of September 1992, which erupted despite the unusually strong incentive participating governments had to remain committed to their EMS parities (in view of the impending French referendum on the Maastricht Treaty and their desire to qualify for participation in EMU) is taken as proof of this point. The only solution to this problem, the argument concludes, is an institutional innovation, namely, a European central bank, that removes the option of reneging and guarantees that exchange rates have been fixed once and for all.[6]

This conclusion has not been universally accepted. Neumann (1992), for one, suggests that a sufficiently credible commitment to intra-EC exchange-rate stability by the existing European central banks could fix exchange rates even in the absence of capital controls.[7] Capital will move in stabilizing rather than destabilizing directions if speculators believe the authorities' stated commitment to defend the rate, as shown by the recent literature on exchange-rate target zones (Flood, Rose, and Mathieson, 1991). By this interpretation, the September 1992 crisis simply reflected the fact that governments' commitments to their pegged exchange rates remain incomplete.

Given the difficulty of drawing inferences from such recent events, it is worth considering the nineteenth-century gold standard, the last regime under which the exchange rates of the major industrial countries were stabilized within narrow bands. The commitment of the major European countries to their gold-standard parities was regarded as credible, so capital flowed to countries whose exchange rates were temporarily weak, thereby stabilizing intra-European parities.[8] Exchange-rate stability minimized uncertainty and transactions costs,

[6] As the authors of the Delors Report put the point, "A new monetary institution . . . [is] needed because a single monetary policy cannot result from independent actions by different national central banks" (Committee, 1989, p. 32).

[7] Gros and Thygesen (1992, pp. 163-194) similarly argue that speculative attacks can be rebuffed if the authorities remain committed to monetary policies that are consistent in the long run with their exchange-rate target.

[8] For details, see Eichengreen (1992b). Flood, Rose, and Mathieson (1991) show that the classical gold standard more closely resembles a well-behaved target zone than do subsequent pegged-rate systems.

deepening the integration of international financial markets, as evidenced by the small size of international interest differentials and the large magnitude of international capital flows (McKinnon, 1993). To this extent, gold-standard experience is consistent with Neumann's conclusion that full monetary union is not needed to reap the benefits of market integration.

The credibility of exchange-rate commitments under the nineteenth-century gold standard was supported, however, by special circumstances not present today. The limited extent of the franchise and private-sector status of the leading European central banks insulated monetary policymakers from political pressures. Even where such pressures might perhaps have been applied, the incentive to influence the banks was limited because the connections between monetary policy and domestic macroeconomic conditions were imperfectly appreciated. The situation was different in Latin America and the United States. In Latin America, the gold-standard years were marked by recurrent bouts of exchange-rate instability, as coalitions of debtors and exporters pressed for the adoption of cheap-money policies. In the United States, the commitment to the gold standard was called into question in the 1890s, when the inflationist free-silver movement peaked and William Jennings Bryan campaigned for the presidency. The operation of the North Atlantic capital market was disrupted, and large interest differentials emerged between assets denominated in sterling and dollars.

Past experience thus suggests that many of the benefits of currency unification can in principle be reaped through the maintenance of firmly fixed exchange rates between distinct national currencies. Experience also suggests, however, that the special circumstances conferring credibility to governments' commitments to fixed rates in earlier years are not present in Europe today.

3 COSTS OF MONETARY UNIFICATION FOR EUROPE

The Incidence and Magnitude of Shocks

Why should countries value the option of changing the exchange rate? The textbook answer (Mundell, 1963; Fleming, 1962) is that exchange-rate changes allowing for independent monetary (and perhaps also fiscal) policies aid the pursuit of full employment. An asymmetric shock (a shift in demand from domestic to foreign products, for example) requires an adjustment in domestic costs (in this case, a reduction) to restore prices and demand to levels consistent with full employment. Changing the exchange rate may be a relatively efficient way of accomplishing this in a decentralized market. This is the "daylight-savings-time" argument for exchange-rate changes.

The value of changing the exchange rate depends, therefore, on the extent of asymmetric shocks. Bayoumi and Eichengreen (1993c) compare the correlation of output fluctuations and inflation rates across EC countries and U.S. regions. For U.S. regions, the option value of changing the exchange rate is dominated by the efficiency of a common currency, or so revealed-preference arguments suggest; the United States therefore provides an obvious metric for gauging the European case. The correlations of GDP growth rates of other EC members with Germany's growth rate over the last thirty years average 0.58, whereas the correlations of growth rates of U.S. regions with that for the U.S. mid-eastern region average 0.68.[9] These correlations for European countries and U.S. regions are displayed in Figure 2. Note the difference between the scales in the two panels, which is indicative of the higher correlations within the United States.

Movements in output growth rates are not the same thing as shocks, for fluctuations in growth rates reflect both disturbances and subsequent adjustments. The technique of Blanchard and Quah (1989) can be used, however, to recover temporary and permanent disturbances from time series of output and prices. This involves transforming the residuals from regressions of growth and inflation rates on lagged values of themselves,

[9] These are unweighted averages from Bayoumi's and Eichengreen's (1993c) table 1. Germany and the mid-eastern region of the United States are treated as the center or "anchor" regions of the respective economic groups.

FIGURE 2

CORRELATION OF GROWTH AND INFLATION RATES WITH ANCHOR COUNTRY OR U.S. REGION

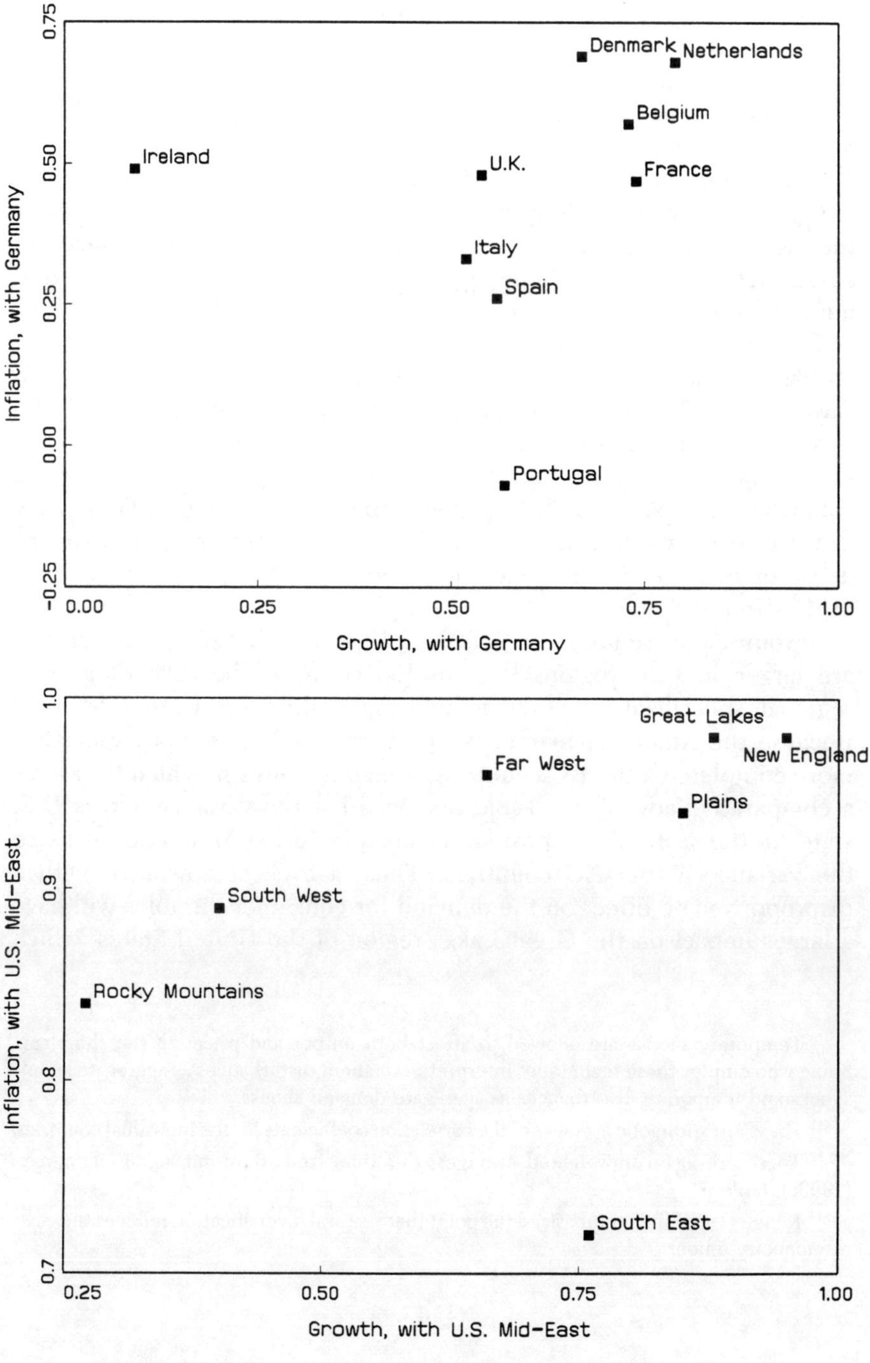

subject to the assumption that permanent disturbances affect both output and price levels in the long run but that temporary disturbances have no long-run output effect.[10] Using this procedure, the correlations of the permanent disturbances of other EC countries with those of Germany averages only 0.33, compared to 0.46 in the United States; the correlations of the temporary disturbances of other EC countries with those of Germany averages only 0.18, compared to 0.37 in the United States.[11]

Correlation coefficients for individual countries and regions are shown in Figure 3. That shocks in Europe are relatively idiosyncratic strengthens the case for policy autonomy, enhancing the option value of separate currencies. Other things being equal, it suggests that Europe may find it more difficult to operate a monetary union than does the United States.

The same methodology can be used to estimate the magnitude of shocks, another criterion for gauging the value of policy autonomy (see Bayoumi, 1992). Here the evidence is less clear-cut. Permanent disturbances are larger for EC countries than for U.S. regions, reinforcing the preceding conclusion. Their standard deviation is 2.1 percent for EC countries, compared to 1.5 percent for U.S. regions.[12] Temporary disturbances, by contrast, are smaller for EC countries; their standard deviation averages 1.7 percent, compared to 2.1 percent for the regions of the United States.

Bayoumi and Eichengreen (1993c) conjecture that temporary shocks are larger in U.S. regions than in EC countries because of greater regional specialization of manufacturing within the United States.[13] Because the American market is so integrated, U.S. regions specialize more completely than EC countries in manufactures in which they have a comparative advantage. Table 2 shows that the variance across U.S. states in the sectoral composition of manufacturing production is twice the variance across EC countries. Thus, a cyclical downturn with a disproportionate effect on the demand for consumer durables will have a larger impact on the Great Lakes region of the United States, which

[10] Temporary shocks are allowed to affect both output and prices in the short run. Some who employ these techniques interpret permanent disturbances as aggregate supply shocks and temporary disturbances as aggregate demand shocks.

[11] These are arithmetic averages of the correlation coefficients for the individual countries.

[12] These are again unweighted averages, this time from Bayoumi and Eichengreen (1993c), table 6.

[13] Kenen (1969) first emphasized the point that sectoral diversification reduces the costs of monetary union.

FIGURE 3

CORRELATION OF PERMANENT AND TEMPORARY DISTURBANCES WITH ANCHOR COUNTRY OR U.S. REGION

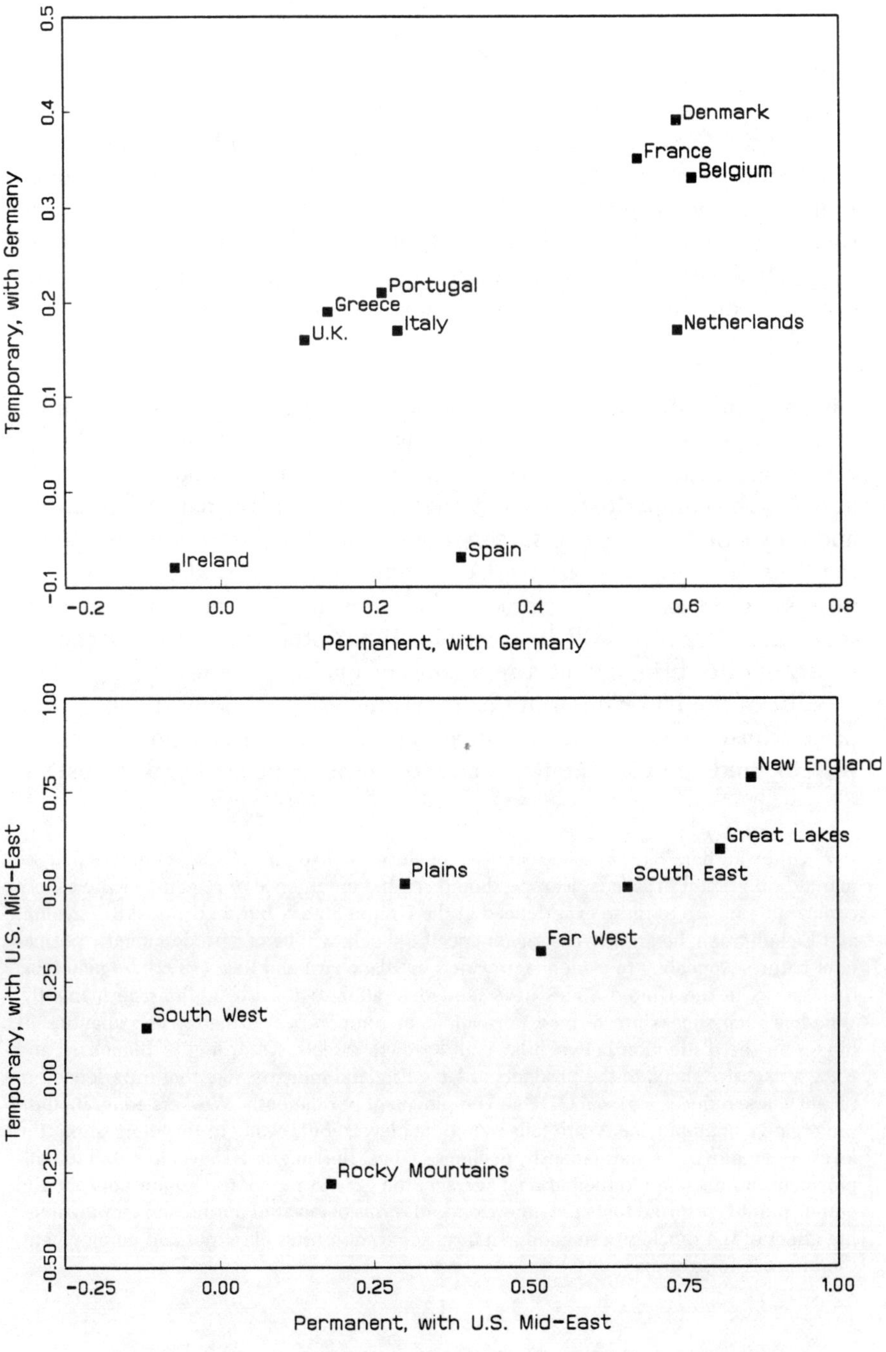

specializes in automobiles and other durable goods, than on analogous European regions. In Europe, transactions costs and government policies support more market segmentation and hence less regional specialization. Less regional specialization diminishes the magnitude of temporary region-specific shocks.

But regional specialization will increase with the completion of the 1992 Program, amplifying region-specific shocks.[14] It is often argued that, under EMU, monetary and fiscal policies will be increasingly synchronized across European countries, eliminating policy-induced region-specific disturbances. The literature on regional specialization points out, however, that important forces work in the opposite direction. These will tend to increase the cost of eliminating use of the exchange rate as an instrument of adjustment.

Speed of Adjustment

Imagine that demand shifts away from products of a particular country and unemployment there consequently rises. If changing the exchange rate is an option, policymakers can devalue the national currency to enhance the competitiveness of domestic goods on international markets, and they can initiate expansionary policies to stimulate domestic spending. But, if European nations, like regions of the United States, do not possess separate currencies, neither devaluation nor independent monetary expansion will be possible. What other mechanisms can be substituted to bring about a reduction of unemployment?

A list of the most important channels includes (1) domestic wage and price adjustments, (2) interregional migration, (3) interregional flows of private and public capital, and (4) interregional fiscal transfers.

[14] Other authors have reached similar conclusions. Krugman (1993) predicts that, as market integration proceeds, Europe should see the emergence of region-specific shocks comparable in size to those experienced in the United States. But, in contrast to Bayoumi and Eichengreen, he argues that region-specific shocks will be of a predominantly permanent nature. Appealing to evidence provided by Blanchard and Katz (1992), he maintains that shocks in the United States have tended to alter regional conditions permanently. Whether such shocks are termed permanent or temporary is a matter of semantics. It hinges on the distinction between level and growth effects. According to Blanchard and Katz, a negative shock to the products of New England industry, like that experienced in recent years, reduces regional GDP and employment permanently. Workers emigrate until the region's unemployment rate falls to national levels, but, owing to this emigration, the level of employment permanently declines. Once the migrants have left and unemployment has declined to the national average, the growth rate of the region's output and employment is restored to its previous trend. In terms of *levels* of output and employment, the effect of the shock is permanent. In terms of *growth rates* of output and employment, the effect is temporary.

TABLE 2
COMPOSITION OF MANUFACTURING PRODUCTION IN THE EC AND THE UNITED STATES
(*percentage points*)

		EC[a]		U.S.	
Sectors	Year	Mean	Variance	Mean	Variance
Food, beverages, and tobacco	1980	11.3	11.2	10.8	15.3
	1989	11.2	11.3	8.3	3.9
Textiles, clothing, and leather	1980	10.0	30.3	6.5	30.0
	1989	8.1	25.9	4.8	15.9
Wood and wood products	1980	4.4	1.6	4.9	8.0
	1989	3.8	1.4	4.3	3.1
Paper and paper products	1980	6.7	6.1	9.8	10.8
	1989	7.4	5.9	8.8	8.6
Chemicals and chemical products	1980	15.7	2.5	14.2	28.3
	1989	17.0	5.8	17.1	33.9
Non-metallic mineral products	1980	5.4	1.1	3.3	0.7
	1989	4.8	1.4	2.7	0.3
Basic metals	1980	6.9	4.2	7.5	9.5
	1989	6.2	2.4	4.1	3.7
Metals products (except	1980	9.9	3.9	8.4	4.8
machinery and equipment)	1989	9.3	2.9	7.4	5.0
Machinery (except electrical)	1980	9.3	12.9	13.5	20.3
	1989	10.1	12.9	19.8	27.2
Electrical machinery	1980	9.2	5.3	9.9	6.3
	1989	10.5	8.6	10.3	9.6
Transport equipment	1980	11.2	6.1	11.3	27.8
	1989	11.7	7.5	12.5	26.4
Average[b]	1980	—	8.39	—	16.71
	1989	—	8.38	—	17.97

SOURCE: Bini-Smaghi and Vori (1992).

[a] Luxembourg is excluded from EC aggregates.

[b] The average variances have been computed using the corresponding mean values as weights.

Reduced-form evidence on the operation of these mechanisms can be gleaned from simulations of Bayoumi's and Eichengreen's (1993c) inflation and output growth regressions. The simulated impulse-response functions are shown in Figure 4 for permanent disturbances and in Figure 5 for temporary ones. The faster response of U.S. regions is apparent. In Figure 4, output in most U.S. regions jumps quickly to its new long-run level; that of the EC countries climbs much more gradually. In Figure 5, where output rises initially in response to a temporary shock but then falls back (by construction), the more gradual response

FIGURE 4

SPEED OF ADJUSTMENT: SIMULATED IMPULSE-RESPONSE FUNCTIONS FOR PERMANENT DISTURBANCES

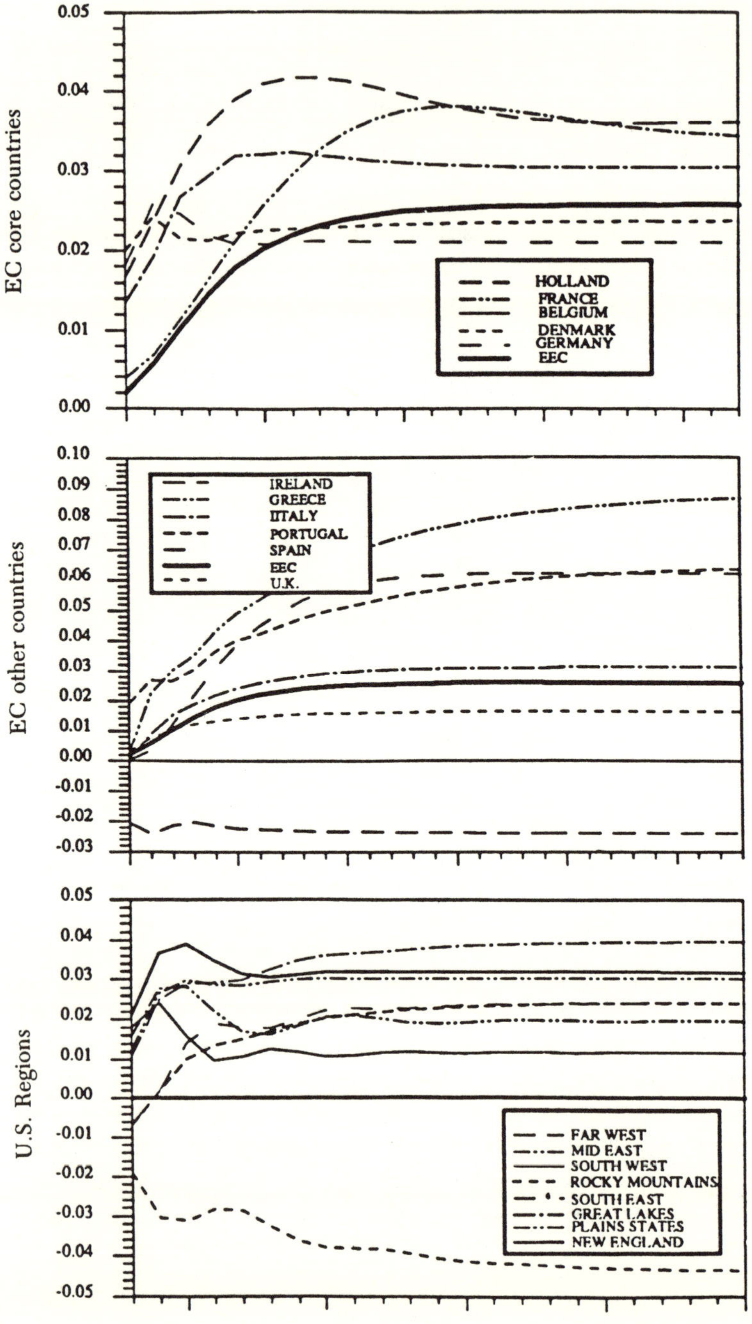

FIGURE 5

SPEED OF ADJUSTMENT: SIMULATED IMPULSE-RESPONSE FUNCTIONS FOR TEMPORARY DISTURBANCES

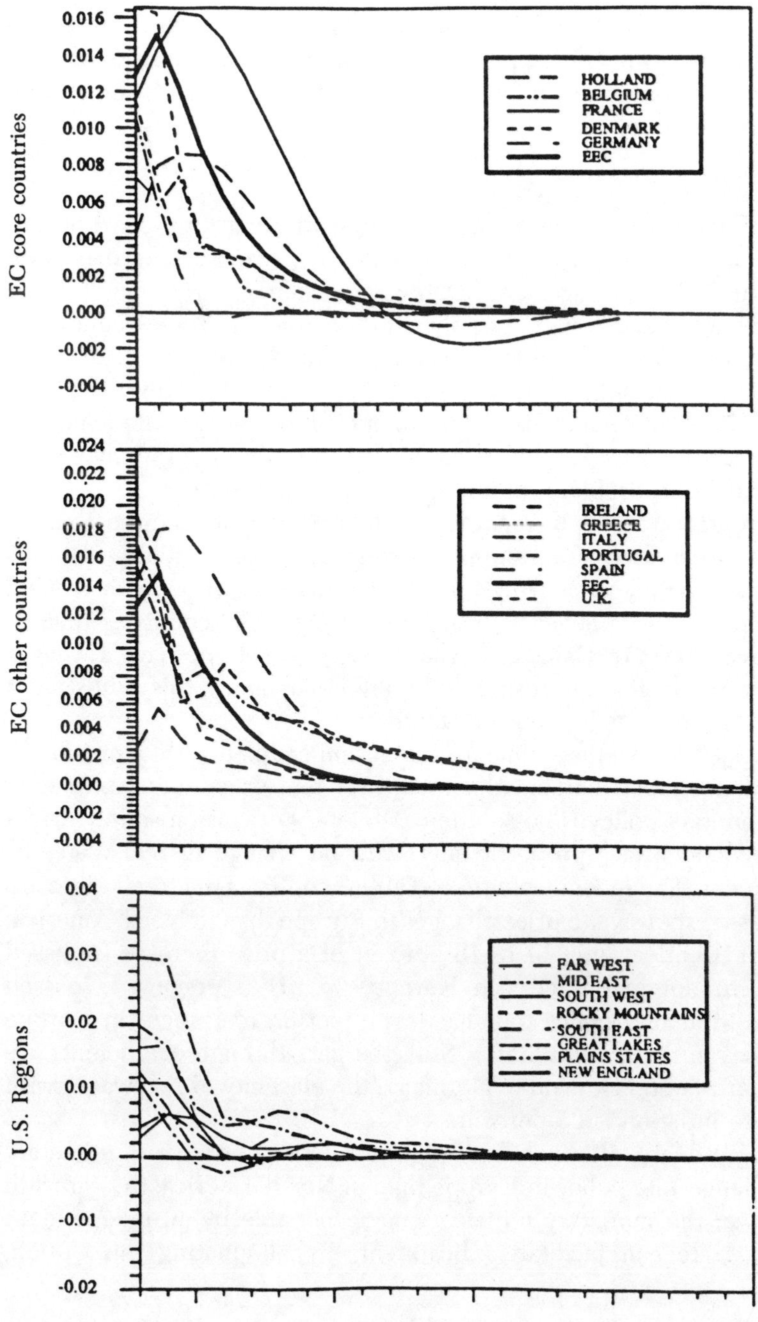

of the EC countries is again evident. Not only are shocks less correlated in Europe than in the United States, but responses are more sluggish.

One might argue that barriers to adjustment will be eroded by EMU and by the rest of the 1992 Program, rendering Europe more similar to the United States in this respect. To evaluate this hypothesis, one must consider the impact of economic and monetary union on each adjustment mechanism in turn.

Wage Adjustments

The textbook prescription for an economy suffering a negative output shock is a reduction in real wages so as to price workers back into employment. If real wages are flexible, labor markets will complete the necessary adjustments without policy intervention. In some economies, however, concern about relative wages, defined over time and across workers, may prevent real wages from adjusting quickly. This is the basis for the "daylight-savings-time" argument for exchange-rate changes. Jumping up the price level by depreciating the exchange rate may solve the coordination problem inhibiting real-wage adjustment.

Real wages are widely regarded as less flexible in Europe than in North America (see, for example, Bruno and Sachs, 1985). Table 3 summarizes evidence showing that the elasticity of wages with respect to unemployment is lower in every one of eight EC countries than in the United States or Canada. Because wages in Europe have a weaker tendency to decline in response to unemployment, this adjustment mechanism operates less powerfully there.

But does it follow that monetary expansion coupled with depreciation can facilitate labor-market adjustment? If real wages are completely rigid, monetary policy is no solution. Monetary expansion simply drives up wages and prices proportionally, with no change in real wages or employment. The second column of Table 3 confirms that real wages are in fact less responsive to price changes in Europe than in North America. In North America, only 14 to 18 percent of a price increase is passed through to nominal wages; in Europe, 25 to 75 percent is passed through. Monetary policy thus has less effect on real wages in Europe than it has in the United States. Still, the pass-through coefficients are all smaller than unity; even in Germany, the elasticity of real wages with respect to inflation is 25 percent.

To recapitulate, although real wages are less responsive to monetary and exchange-rate policy in Europe than in North America, they are still responsive; the monetary initiatives made possible by an independent exchange rate can facilitate adjustment. By eliminating this option,

TABLE 3

SUMMARY MEASURES OF WAGE FLEXIBILITY

	Elasticity of Nominal Wage with Respect to	
Country	Unemployment Rate	Prices
Belgium	−0.25	0.25
Denmark	−0.10	0.25
France	−0.29	0.50
Germany	−0.11	0.75
Italy	−0.39	0.60
Netherlands	−0.27	0.50
Spain	−0.20	0.25
United Kingdom	−0.15	0.33
United States	−0.61	0.14
Canada	−0.51	0.18
Japan	−1.87	0.66

SOURCE: Bini-Smaghi and Vori, 1992; based on OECD, 1989.

monetary unification will leave European labor markets on their own. That wages are adjusted to macroeconomic shocks less skillfully in these markets than in existing monetary unions like the United States and Canada implies that sacrificing monetary autonomy will be more costly.

It can perhaps be argued that European wages have exhibited such inflexibility precisely because of labor's awareness that adjustment can take place on other fronts, notably through changes in exchange rates and monetary or fiscal policies. Eliminating these other margins of adjustment may force workers to accept greater wage flexibility.

German economic and monetary unification (GEMU) in 1990-91 provides a test of this hypothesis. GEMU eliminated the option of using the exchange rate to adjust relative labor costs in the two halves of Germany. Under the hypothesis being considered, higher levels of unemployment in the eastern *lander*, in conjunction with removal of the exchange rate as an adjustment mechanism, should have prompted wage reductions for eastern workers. Instead, German unions pushed for increases with the explicit goal of achieving wage parity between east and west within five years. One motive was the fear that wage reductions in the east would undermine the wage standards in the west. Another was concern that low wages in the east would unleash a socially disruptive migration to the west.

Thus, GEMU lends no support for the hypothesis that monetary union will necessarily enhance relative wage flexibility. One can indeed imagine that the concerns activated by GEMU will operate even more powerfully at the EC level (Doyle, 1989). Labor leaders and government officials may therefore work hard to limit adjustment through wage flexibility.

Interregional Migration

According to Mundell's (1961) seminal article on optimum-currency areas, two nations or regions that experience different disturbances may nevertheless wish to share a common currency so long as labor is mobile between them. Imagine that demand shifts from the products of one member of a monetary union to the products of another. The consequent rise in unemployment in the depressed area will be minimized insofar as labor flows to the booming region. The benefits of a common currency may, under these circumstances, exceed the costs.

There is reason to doubt that adjustment to regional disturbances following EMU will be accomplished through American-style labor mobility. United States experience demonstrates that the effects of barriers to the movement of labor, even when formally dismantled, can persist for decades (Wright, 1986). Although border controls and other statutory restrictions on European labor flows will be eliminated by the 1992 Program, cultural and linguistic barriers will remain.

In contrast to the situation confronting potential migrants *between* European countries, there are no formal barriers to migration *within* those countries. Cultural and linguistic impediments to migration within Britain or Italy should be minor compared to the obstacles to migration between them. Indeed, migration rates within European countries are higher than migration rates between them (De Grauwe and Vanhaverbeke, 1991). By U.S. standards, however, labor mobility is low even within European countries. In 1980, for example, 6.2 percent of the U.S. population changed its county of residence, 3.3 percent its state of residence. In contrast, only 1.1 percent of the English and Welsh population moved between standard census regions, and only 1.3 percent of the German population moved between *lander* (Eichengreen, 1992c). Interregional mobility is even lower in Southern European countries such as Italy and Spain.

Interregional migration data may reflect incentives to move, rather than the willingness to do so. If shocks to U.S. regions are larger and less correlated than shocks to regions within European countries, the larger observed flows of workers within the United States may not reflect greater intrinsic mobility. In Eichengreen (1993a), I therefore estimated migration equations for Britain, Italy, and the United States, relating labor flows to the incentive to move, as represented by relative wage and unemployment rates. Only if the elasticity of interregional migration with respect to these variables differs across countries is it safe to conclude that labor mobility differs.

The framework for this analysis is the Pissarides-McMaster (1990) migration model for Britain. As in their paper, I find that immigration responds positively to changes in local wages relative to national wages and negatively to local unemployment relative to national unemployment. (See column one of Table 4.) Migratory patterns are persistent, as reflected in the coefficient on the lagged dependent variable.[15]

The second column presents estimates for nine U.S. regions. Although most coefficients have the same signs and significance levels as in the British equation, the elasticity of immigration with respect to the change in relative wages is an order of magnitude larger. The elasticity with respect to relative unemployment rates is twice as large. In contrast to the British result, moreover, there is little persistence in U.S. migratory patterns after controlling for wage and unemployment differentials. This suggests that migration is more responsive to current economic conditions in the United States.

Turning to Italy, neither the change in relative wages (the compensation of all employees, inclusive of social-security contributions) nor relative unemployment has much impact on migration, which displays even more persistence than in Britain. One might conclude on this basis that Italian labor is unresponsive to these variables. But, as Attanasio and Padoa Schioppa (1991) and A'Hearn (1991) show, explanatory power can be enhanced by substituting the level of the wage differential for its first difference. Column four of Table 4 displays this variant of the model. Both relative wages and relative unemployment affect migration as expected. But, compared to the United States, migration is more persistent and less responsive to unemployment differentials.

As labor mobility within countries may be regarded as an upper bound on mobility between them, there is little reason to expect that it will play a role in post-EMU Europe as important as in the United States.

Interregional Capital Flows

Even if labor fails to flow out of depressed regions, capital can flow in, stabilizing economic activity. The very stability of exchange rates within a monetary union encourages capital mobility by reducing risk.

[15] The only respect in which my estimates differ from those of Pissarides and McMaster is in the coefficient on relative wages. My point estimate is smaller than theirs and is statistically different from zero at the 90- rather than the 95-percent level.

TABLE 4

MIGRATION MODELS FOR BRITAIN, THE UNITED STATES, AND ITALY

(dependent variable is immigration scaled by population)

	(1) Britain 1961-82	(2) United States 1962-88	(3) Italy 1962-85	(4) Italy 1962-85
Constant	0.12	1.50	0.01	0.37
	(2.32)	(5.76)	(5.76)	(2.70)
Change in log wages lagged	0.42	15.13	0.22	—
	(1.76)	(2.52)	(0.45)	—
Level of log wages lagged	—	—	—	1.07
	—	—	—	(4.43)
Unemployment lagged	-0.17	-0.37	-0.04	-0.02
	(2.87)	(1.92)	(0.50)	(2.31)
Migration lagged	0.58	-0.05	0.73	0.62
	(9.56)	(0.77)	(21.98)	(16.01)
N	180	243	144	144

NOTE: *t*-statistics are in parentheses. Changes in wage and unemployment variables denote ratios of local value to national average. Dummy variables for regions are included in each regression but are not reported.

Eichengreen (1990) shows that capital flows initiated in response to disturbances to a region's balance of payments operate more powerfully within the United States than across EC countries. When California's balance of payments weakens and the loss of domestic credit raises interest rates, capital flows into the state to take advantage of the incipient interest differential, financing the payments imbalance. But, when Portugal's balance of payments deteriorates, the risk of currency devaluation limits the capital inflow. Domestic interest rates rise, crowding out investment.

The increased capital mobility that will result from the removal of exchange controls and the rest of the Single Market Program, in conjunction with the elimination of exchange risk if monetary union is achieved, will cause capital mobility in the EC to resemble more closely capital mobility within the United States. When Portugal's balance of payments weakens, capital will flow in more readily, preventing Portuguese interest rates from rising relative to those elsewhere in the EC. But, unlike California, Portugal, as a sovereign nation, will retain the option of seceding from the EC, reestablishing a national currency, and devaluing. Thus, some devaluation risk, however small, will remain to discourage capital flows.

Whereas stabilizing capital inflows are likely to be forthcoming in response to balance-of-payments shocks, they are less likely to be provided in response to the problems of a depressed region. When a region, be it California or Portugal, experiences a depression relative to its neighbors, local demands for credit and capital decline. Interest rates will fall rather than rise, leaving capital no incentive to flow in. Idle labor may be abundant in the depressed region, but it is not cheap, barring significant wage adjustments. Hence, the shock to the regional economy that produced the slump in output and employment will limit capital inflows. Blanchard and Katz (1992) document that capital movements into depressed regions play only a minor role in regional adjustment in the United States.

4 FISCAL POLICY AND EMU

Excessive or Inadequate Government Borrowing?

Might government borrowing substitute for private borrowing? Governments of European countries suffering temporary declines in demand can bolster domestic spending by running budget deficits. So long as the sovereign borrower is expected to pay the money back, capital will flow in to finance its budget deficits, sustaining economic activity. Discretionary fiscal policy can thus substitute for monetary-cum-exchange-rate policy in a monetary union.

Yet, the capacity of European governments to run budget deficits and borrow externally will be reduced by the rise in factor mobility associated with the 1992 Program. Theoretical models such as that of Glick and Hutchinson (1992) show that high capital mobility in conjunction with fixed exchange rates (or monetary union) tighten the government budget constraint. Government borrowing today is limited by the taxes that can be levied tomorrow (taxes to be used to service the accumulated debt). If capital and labor are freely mobile within the currency union, borrowing today—which implies higher taxes tomorrow—may induce mobile factors of production to flee to lower-tax jurisdictions, thereby eroding the local tax base. As investors understand that a government's ability to borrow today is limited by its ability to tax tomorrow, and that its ability to tax tomorrow is limited by factor mobility, they will refuse to lend to a government attempting to exceed its capacity to borrow. The higher capital mobility is, the sooner this will occur.

Evidence from the U.S. state and municipal bond markets suggests that market discipline is indeed operative. Bayoumi, Goldstein, and Woglom (1992), employing a sample of state and municipal bonds, find that state and local governments are rationed out of capital markets when the debt-to-gross-state-product ratio exceeds 8 percent. There is no reason to think that market discipline would become binding at equally low levels in an integrated Europe, for, as just described, the mobility of some factors of production, notably labor, is likely to remain lower than in the United States. And, even within the United States, factor mobility, although encouraging tax convergence, does not require tax equalization. All factors of production do not flee from Massachusetts to New Hampshire, for example, because New Hampshire has no income tax. The incentive to migrate is limited by relocation costs; in addition, it is diminished by the capitalization in housing prices of differences in local services and tax burdens (Bayoumi and Gordon, 1991). The elasticity of factor flows with respect to tax differentials is positive but not infinite. Because states retain some scope for levying different tax rates, they can service different levels of debt and hence run different deficits. Even if mobility is less than perfect, however, the increased mobility of factors produced by completion of the Single Market Program will tighten the constraints on fiscal policy. It may limit deficit spending for stabilization purposes more than European governments desire.[16] From the standpoint of stabilization, fiscal policy may thus prove to be an imperfect substitute for the relinquished monetary instrument.

Debate in Europe focuses, however, not on whether post-EMU governments will have adequate freedom to vary fiscal policy over the cycle, but on whether economic and monetary integration will induce excessive deficit spending, irrespective of cyclical conditions. This problem is analyzed by Canzoneri and Diba (1991). They assume that deficit spending leads to the accumulation of debt that must be serviced through the imposition of distortionary taxes. If capital is not mobile internationally, that debt will be held at home; only domestic interest rates will rise as a result of additional public spending, and only domestic residents will suffer additional distortionary taxation. A government wishing to maximize domestic welfare will take into account the consequences of the future distortionary taxation implied by its current spending and will set the level of government expenditure accordingly. Once financial markets become integrated internationally as a result of economic union, however, interest rates will move together at home and abroad. Deficit spending that drives up interest rates at home will drive up interest rates abroad as investors shift from low- to higher-yield assets.[17] Hence, some of the costs of additional spending by the domestic government will be borne by foreign residents, as foreign governments will also be forced to levy additional distortionary taxes to pay the higher interest charges on their outstanding debt. In a noncooperative

[16] The same can be said of local jurisdictions within existing monetary unions like the United States. As we shall see below, however, there exist in these unions alternative sources of fiscal flexibility, such as fiscal federalism.

[17] Note that this effect follows from the substitutability of domestic and foreign assets in investors' portfolios, not from any failure of markets to properly price the risk of default by heavily indebted governments.

equilibrium, public spending will be too high as a result of economic integration.[18]

When monetary union is added to the analysis, member states may have an even stronger incentive to spend and borrow excessively, insofar as they can anticipate a bailout from the new monetary authority. Imagine a situation, once more following Canzoneri and Diba (1991), where a state has spent excessively and is confronted with the need to impose costly distortionary taxes. In deciding the amount of seigniorage revenue to contribute to that state's budget, the central bank will solve the Ramsey-Phelps optimal taxation problem, equalizing on the margin the costs of distortionary taxes and of seigniorage revenues (where the cost of additional seigniorage is the deadweight loss associated with the reduction in agents' holdings of real-money balances due to inflation). Faced with a government engaged in high levels of spending, it will create additional inflation, bailing out the fiscal authorities with purchases of debt financed by money creation.

Although this same problem arises in the presence of national central banks, it is more severe in a monetary union, where a single central bank serves several national governments. In a monetary union, some of the deadweight loss associated with seigniorage will be borne by the residents of other states, a fact that will encourage state governments to reduce distortionary taxes and finance their deficits with additional seigniorage. (Because the seigniorage is spread over a larger number of agents, its marginal cost is lower; an optimizing government will reduce distortionary taxes to match this marginal cost.) If the governments of several member states play this game noncooperatively, each will increase its deficit spending in an effort to secure a larger share of the seigniorage revenue provided by the central bank, producing not only larger overall deficits, but also higher levels of inflation.

These problems are well known from the literature on international policy coordination and are best solved by coordinated reductions in

[18] A possible objection to this analysis is that it is based on overly strong assumptions about international transmission. In the model from which this discussion is drawn, Canzoneri and Diba (1991) assume perfect substitutability of goods produced at home and abroad. In alternative models with imperfect substitutability (namely, van der Ploeg, 1989), fiscal policy in noncooperative equilibrium may be inadequately, rather than excessively, expansionary. If fiscal expansion leads to real appreciation (as it will upon relaxing the assumption of perfect substitutability), it will stimulate exports and increase employment in neighboring countries, swamping the negative effect of higher interest rates. But empirical studies (Roubini, 1989; Masson and Melitz, 1991) suggest that fiscal spillovers are predominantly negative; the interest-rate effects emphasized in the text dominate.

government spending. Article 103 of the Maastricht Treaty instructs member states to "coordinate [their economic policies] within the Council [of Ministers]." The Council, acting by a qualified majority on a recommendation from the Commission, may draft guidelines for the economic policies of member countries and report its findings to the European Council. It will then monitor developments in member countries and make recommendations to national governments in the event that the latters' policies are inconsistent with those guidelines. If countries fail to respond appropriately, the Council may recommend that the European Investment Bank halt lending to the country, require it to make non-interest-bearing deposits with the Community, and impose unspecified fines.

The issue is whether these relatively weak sanctions will suffice to compel intra-EMU coordination or whether more formal restraints on fiscal policies are required. The Delors Report (Committee, 1989, p. 30) insisted that, "in the budgetary field, binding rules are required that would . . . impose effective upper limits on budget deficits of individual member countries. . . ." According to Article 104 of the Maastricht Treaty, in Stage II of the transition to EMU (when domestic economic policies converge in anticipation of the irrevocable locking of exchange rates), governments will be required to limit their budget deficits to 3 percent of GDP and to reduce their debts to 60 percent of GDP. In Stage III, when the European Central Bank (ECB) comes into operation, the treaty binds national governments not to run excessive deficits, although it does not provide numerical thresholds like those of Stage II.

These debt and deficit rules raise two questions. One is whether such fiscal restraints are effective. Article 104 is qualified by loopholes. For example, excessive deficits will only be said to exist if the deficit ratio exceeds 3 percent and if, *in addition*, either it has not declined "substantially and continuously" to "close to" that level or it cannot be regarded as "exceptional and temporary and . . . close to" the 3-percent threshold. The debt ratio will be said to be excessive only if it exceeds 60 percent and if, *in addition*, it is not "sufficiently diminishing and approaching the 60-percent level at a satisfactory pace."[19] The U.S. states, which are subject to fiscal restraints featuring similar loopholes, are sometimes said to be able to evade them easily.

The other question is whether such restraints are desirable. If effectively enforced, will the fiscal policies they produce approximate those that would result from international policy coordination? Before

[19] It is relevant that early drafts of the treaty referred to fiscal ceilings, whereas the final version substituted the term "reference values."

considering this second question in Chapter 7, I turn to the first, whether such fiscal restraints are effective.

The Debate Over Fiscal Restraints

Fiscal restraints are widespread in existing monetary unions. Two types of self-imposed restraints are prevalent in the United States: so-called balanced-budget requirements limiting the deficits that state governments can run, and public-debt ceilings limiting the debts that states can accumulate. As of 1987, forty-six states had balanced-budget requirements of some sort, while the constitutions of some thirty states limited the power to issue debt.

It is not obvious that these restrictions, whether statutory or constitutional, actually limit the deficits or debts they are designed to control or that either type of restriction reduces the interest rate the state must pay to borrow. Most studies conclude that fiscal restraints have little if any impact on fiscal performance. Von Hagen (1991), for example, compares levels of state debt per capita and debt-to-income ratios in states with and without debt limits, finding that the differences between the two groups are statistically insignificant. He also finds that balanced-budget requirements do not have a statistically significant impact on state debt per capita.

There are good reasons to reconsider this question. Most work on the issue, including that of von Hagen, employs bivariate tests that compare the level of debt in states with and without fiscal restraints without controlling for other determinants. Two recent studies that used a multivariate framework (ACIR, 1987; Goldstein and Woglom, 1992) in fact reported statistically significant effects of fiscal restraints.

I analyze pooled time-series-cross-section data for the fifty states for the years 1985 through 1989 (the most recent five years for which data were available at the time of writing; further details and regression results may be found in Eichengreen, 1993b.) Following the Advisory Commission on Intergovernmental Relations (ACIR, 1987), I relate the general fund surplus or deficit per capita to agricultural output per capita (Agripc), the percentage of state population aged 65 or older (Elders), federal aid to the state per capita (Grant), and a dummy variable for southern states (South). Grants should enter with a positive sign insofar as they permit politicians to replace deficit spending with spending out of federal aid. The dummy variable for southern states should enter negatively if the region, as sometimes asserted, is fiscally conservative. Agricultural output should similarly display a negative sign if farm states are fiscally conservative.

TABLE 5
THE EFFECT OF FISCAL RESTRAINTS ON THE GENERAL-FUND BUDGET BALANCE

	(1)	(2)	(3)
Constant	46.23	25.30	41.93
	(1.02)	(0.52)	(1.10)
Balance 1	23.43	—	—
	(2.06)	—	—
Balance 2	—	3.16	—
	—	(1.63)	—
Balance 3	—	—	19.65
	—	—	(2.13)
Elders	-2.08	-1.48	-5.01
	(-0.74)	(-0.53)	(-2.05)
Grant	0.02	0.02	0.12
	(0.37)	(0.46)	(3.15)
South	-40.38	-36.45	-28.38
	(-2.91)	(-2.67)	(-2.55)
Agripc	0.01	0.01	0.01
	(1.31)	(1.18)	(1.56)
1986	-10.92	-11.12	-12.94
	(-0.56)	(0.66)	(-0.92)
1987	-2.92	0.17	-9.21
	(-0.17)	(0.03)	(-0.64)
1988	18.53	19.60	2.37
	(1.10)	(1.16)	(0.17)
1989	29.21	26.74	15.56
	(1.71)	(1.56)	(1.10)
N	250	250	242
R-squared	0.09	0.08	0.14
F-statistic	2.58	2.39	5.34

NOTE: *t*-statistics are in parentheses.

The signs of the coefficients, shown in Table 5, are as predicted, although statistical significance varies. Most important, a number of measures of balanced-budget restrictions are significantly associated with larger surpluses (smaller deficits).[20] The first such measure is a dummy variable equalling 1 for states prohibited from carrying a deficit into the next fiscal year (Balance 1). The second is an index (ranging from 1 to 10) constructed to capture the relative stringency of state balanced-

[20] Fiscal restrictions are themselves largely exogenous with respect to current-account deficits and debts, because these statutory and constitutional provisions generally date from the nineteenth century, when they were adopted in response to debt defaults occurring for reasons unrelated to economic structures and conditions today.

budget requirements (Balance 2). The third is a dummy variable equalling 1 for states the governors of which must sign a balanced budget by statutory or constitutional law (Balance 3). Balance 1 and Balance 3 both display significant effects.

Table 6 turns from balanced-budget requirements to debt limits, again employing a variant of the ACIR specification. The dependent variable is state government long-term debt per capita. The results indicate that constitutional debt limits (Dbtlim) exert a downward influence on state debts.[21] The point estimate of −250 implies that their presence reduces state debt per capita by $250.

Table 7 shifts the focus from quantities to prices. It considers the impact of debt and deficit limits on the yields on state bonds (rather than on stock or flow supplies). I use the data recently obtained by Goldstein and Woglom (1992) on yields borne by state general obligations. The dependent variable is the difference in basis points between the yield on twenty-year general-obligation bonds for a specific date and that on a twenty-year New Jersey general obligation bond for the same date, again for the years 1985 through 1989. The debt-limit variable is consistently indistinguishable from zero. Thus, although debt limits influence the quantity of debt outstanding, it is less clear that they influence the required rate of return. (This would follow if the quantity of debt is not an important predictor of default.) The balanced-budget variables, in the remaining columns, generally have a significant negative impact on yields. In contrast to debt limits, then, balanced-budget requirements significantly affect both yields and borrowing.[22] Thus, the results for U.S. states generally confirm the contention that fiscal restraints can significantly affect fiscal outcomes.

The Debate Over Fiscal Federalism

When borrowing by states within a monetary union throws off negative externalities and must therefore be restrained, or the mobility of factors of production within the union limits the borrowing capacity of state and local jurisdictions, there may be need for alternative mechanisms to transfer resources to depressed regions. Sachs and Sala-i-Martin (1990)

[21] The dependent variable is measured as long-term debt outstanding minus long-term debt offsets. I also analyzed full-faith-and-credit long-term debt and nonguaranteed long-term debt to test whether debt limits led states to substitute the latter for the former. I found no evidence of this; debt limits had negative effects on both types of debt.

[22] This is plausible if default risk increases with the rate of growth of the debt rather than with its average level.

TABLE 6

THE EFFECT OF FISCAL RESTRAINTS ON LEVELS OF DEBT

	(1)	(2)	(3)
Constant	964.39	-1153.35	-1084.98
	(2.26)	(-1.45)	(-1.39)
Dbtlim	-293.95	-255.19	-224.90
	(-3.11)	(-2.81)	(-2.53)
Elders	-107.23	-53.51	-34.47
	(-5.39)	(2.54)	(-1.61)
Grant	—	1.57	1.66
	—	(5.11)	(5.60)
Item	—	-147.69	-85.16
	—	(-1.26)	(-0.73)
Size	—	-1.88	-2.32
	—	(-2.45)	(-3.06)
South	-62.78	282.96	201.12
	(-0.53)	(2.42)	(1.72)
TEL	—	81.64	24.17
	—	(0.91)	(0.27)
Year	—	0.18	0.22
	—	(0.53)	(0.67)
YPC	0.10	0.15	0.13
	(3.74	(6.36)	(5.34)
Agripc	-0.09	—	-0.15
	(-1.87)	—	(-3.21)
1986	63.62	4.28	5.28
	(0.53)	(0.04)	(0.05)
1987	135.02	66.23	77.34
	(1.09)	(0.58)	(0.69)
1988	-147.80	-301.42	-255.90
	(-1.23)	(-2.46)	(-2.12)
N	200	200	200
R-squared	0.34	0.44	0.47
F-statistic	12.06	12.29	12.69

NOTE: *t*-statistics are in parentheses. For further discussion of the variables "Item" (states having line-item vetoes), "Size" (of state legislature), "TEL" (tax or expenditure limitation), "Year" (of statehood), and "YPC" (state product per capita), see Eichengreen (1993b).

have revived Ingram's (1959) argument that fiscal federalism serves this function in monetary unions like the United States and that its absence from the Maastricht Treaty will complicate regional problems following the transition to EMU. They estimate that the federal fiscal system in the United States, by reducing federal tax liabilities and increasing inward transfers, offsets roughly 35 percent of a state's income loss when

TABLE 7

THE EFFECT OF FISCAL RESTRAINTS ON STATE BOND YIELDS

	(1)	(2)	(3)	(4)
Constant	-14.13	-17.56	-2.51	-11.56
	(-1.23)	(-1.70)	(-0.23)	(-1.02)
Balance 1	—	-12.52	—	—
	—	(-4.75)	—	—
Balance 2	—	—	-1.53	—
	—	—	(-3.62)	—
Balance 3	—	—	—	-0.14
	—	—	—	(-0.05)
Dbtlim	0.16	—	—	—
	(0.06)	—	—	—
Elders	0.94	1.48	1.03	0.73
	(1.43)	(2.39)	(1.66)	(1.05)
Grant	0.04	0.04	0.03	0.04
	(3.72)	(4.56)	(3.53)	(2.73)
South	3.89	9.53	5.87	4.19
	(1.24)	(2.99)	(1.91)	(1.28)
Agripc	0.0002	-0.002	0.0007	0.0008
	(0.12)	(-0.74)	(0.35)	(0.33)
1986	-1.04	-1.35	-0.94	-0.99
	(-0.26)	(-0.35)	(-0.25)	(-0.24)
1987	-0.26	-0.47	-1.92	-0.13
	(-0.06)	(-0.12)	(-0.49)	(-0.03)
1988	-3.26	-3.41	-4.22	-3.41
	(-0.81)	(-0.90)	(-1.08)	(-0.82)
1989	-6.74	-7.27	-5.62	-6.27
	(-1.64)	(-1.89)	(-1.42)	(-1.43)
N	200	200	200	200
R-squared	0.08	0.18	0.14	0.06
F-statistic	1.90	4.63	3.48	1.23

NOTE: *t*-statistics are in parentheses.

it experiences a recession. Purchasing power is stabilized, diminishing the effects of regional problems that can no longer be redressed by changing the exchange rate.

Using data for U.S. census regions, Sachs and Sala-i-Martin fit regressions relating tax and transfer payments to movements in pretax personal income, both measured relative to the national average. (Real energy prices and a time trend are also included as determinants of state tax liabilities, and an effort is made to control for simultaneity due to the dependence of state income on taxes and transfers.) The elasticities from these regressions are then used to infer the size of the stabilization effect on income. They find that federal tax liabilities decline by roughly $0.25 for every dollar by which regional income falls short of national income and that inward transfers rise by roughly $0.10. Thus, stabilization, which is substantial, occurs mainly on the tax side.

These results have not gone unchallenged. Von Hagen (1990) emphasizes the need to distinguish transfers extended in response to temporary declines in state incomes from those extended in response to permanent declines. Most interstate transfers in the United States, he argues, are permanent transfers designed to offset long-standing differences in state incomes, not temporary transfers extended for cyclical reasons. In the jargon of the EC, the federal system in the United States addresses the problem of "cohesion" as much as that of stabilization. Once permanent and temporary transfers are distinguished, he suggests, one finds that transfers extended in response to cyclical fluctuations are relatively small.

Bayoumi and Masson (1991) have addressed this issue by regressing each region's per capita personal income net of taxes and transfers on its per capita personal income inclusive of taxes and transfers. Both regressors are normalized by the analogous national average. This equation measures the relationship between personal income before and after federal fiscal flows, with the slope coefficient capturing the size of the offset. For the United States, the estimated coefficient of 0.80 indicates that, on average, federal fiscal flows reduce regional income inequalities by $0.20 on the dollar. Thus, Bayoumi's and Masson's estimate, although smaller than that of Sachs and Sala-i-Martin, still suggests a substantial stabilization effect.

To get at the different response to temporary and permanent income fluctuations, Bayoumi and Masson estimate the same regression after differencing all variables to remove the trend. Regressions on the differenced data produce a coefficient of 0.72, suggesting that the stabilization of short-term fluctuations, which comes to $0.28 on the dollar, is even stronger than the overall effect. The largest change in coefficients occurs when personal income is adjusted, not for taxes, but for social insurance, transfers, and grants, consistent with the notion that grant and transfer components of federal programs are particularly responsive to the cycle.

Bayoumi's and Masson's results thus suggest that distinguishing the equalization and stabilization functions of the U.S. federal fiscal system fails to overturn the conclusion reached by Sachs and Sala-i-Martin. Von Hagen's criticism may still be valid for other federal systems, however. The tendency for federal fiscal systems to provide income equalization is likely to be prominent in Canada, for example, where the constitution is generally interpreted as demanding regional equalization of income differentials. Thus, the Canadian case is particularly relevant to Europe, where priority is attached to "cohesion" among EC members and a number of EC countries—notably Germany—have federal constitutions and tax systems with broadly similar features.

As these facts would lead one to expect, Bayoumi's and Masson's analysis for Canada yields evidence of a substantial response to permanent income differentials. Personal direct taxes provide an estimated $0.05 on the dollar of redistribution, while transfers and grants provide $0.15 each. The offset to long-term income differentials is therefore 35 percent, nearly twice the estimate for the United States. The response in Canada to short-term personal income fluctuations is smaller—almost exactly half the response to long-term differentials. Thus, equalization payments extended in response to long-term rather than temporary income differentials play a larger role in Canada than in the United States. Offsets to temporary income fluctuations, although still substantial, are less important.

Although this research documents the need to distinguish equalization payments designed to moderate persistent income differentials from stabilization or insurance effects, it affirms the importance in existing monetary unions of fiscal transfers extended in response to temporary income fluctuations. Does the EC have the capacity to undertake these transfers? As long as the EC budget remains little more than 1 percent of Community gross national product (GNP), it is hard to see how it could evolve into a fiscal mechanism with the redistributive capacity of the U.S. and Canadian federal budgets. As far back as 1977, the MacDougall Report suggested, on essentially these grounds, that an EC budget of at least 5 percent of Community GNP was needed to ensure the viability of monetary union (Commission, 1977). Federal-government spending as a share of consolidated government expenditure points to the same conclusion. It is 69 percent in Belgium, 64 percent in the United States, 61 percent in Germany, 42 percent in Canada, and 30 percent in Switzerland. By comparison, the EC budget is no more than 5 percent of the consolidated government spending of member countries (Van Rompuy, Abraham, and Heremans, 1991, p. 15). Again, the implication is that the EC budget, as it currently stands, possesses rather limited redistributive capacity.

If the case for fiscal federalism is granted, which EC program should take up the slack? Williamson (1990) has revived a proposal, which can be traced back to the Marjolin Report in 1975, for a Community-wide unemployment insurance system as a means of providing regional coinsurance. This may create a number of problems, however. Consider the following example (from Eichengreen, 1992c). National labor unions seeking to maximize the wage bill set the level of real wages, subject to which firms then choose the level of employment. Unions will accept additional unemployment in exchange for higher wages when their members receive more generous unemployment benefits. If the cost of those benefits is shifted from the national level to the Community, it is no longer a transfer exclusively from employed to unemployed residents of a given country. Hence, the union has an incentive to raise its wage demands, producing even more unemployment. Not only does insurance thereby encourage the very outcome of unemployment, the effects of which it is designed to mitigate, but the magnitude of the distortion increases with the extent of fiscal federalism.

The structure of unemployment-insurance funds in the United States mitigates this problem. Each state administers its own insurance trust fund. States also pay a fraction of their payroll taxes into a Federal Unemployment Trust Fund, from which they are permitted to draw when their own trust funds move into deficit. Significantly, however, states must pay interest on the funds they borrow. This minimizes their capacity to shift the cost of unemployment benefits onto other jurisdictions within the federal system.

The Structural Funds set up by the EC provide another potential conduit for fiscal transfers. Targeted at depressed regions within the Community, these funds were recently doubled in size. Spain and other southern members of the EC have lobbied for expanding them further as a precondition for EMU. However, the principal function of the Structural Funds is to transfer resources to regions where incomes are persistently below the EC average. Structural Fund receipts are inelastic with respect to temporary disturbances. Gordon (1991) estimates that a $1 fall in a member state's per capita income increases Structural Fund transfers by at most $0.01. As the Structural Funds have recently been doubled, one might wish to double this estimate. Unless their administration is fundamentally reformed, however, they are an unlikely source of regional coinsurance. For the Structural Funds to substitute for a U.S.-style fiscal federalism, it would be necessary to increase not only their scale, but also their elasticity with respect to current income fluctuations. This would fundamentally alter their raison d'être, something that the current recipients would resist.

5 MAXIMIZING BENEFITS AND MINIMIZING COSTS OF EMU

Designing the ECB

Inflation performance and central-bank structure vary across countries. The correlation between them suggests that the ECB's design will have implications for monetary-policy outcomes under EMU.

Why is central-bank independence conducive to price stability? One explanation is the political business cycle, the tendency for central banks dependent on the good will of incumbent governments to increase inflation prior to elections in an effort to stimulate demand (Alesina, 1989). Another is the time-consistency problem associated with the work of Kydland and Prescott (1977) and Barro and Gordon (1983). If workers must seal wage bargains before the money supply is set, a central bank with discretionary powers has the incentive to produce a surprise inflation to raise demand, profitability, output, and employment. Workers cognizant of the incentive faced by central bankers will increase their wage demands, neutralizing the employment effects. To achieve their goals, central bankers will have to inflate even more, and workers will raise their wage demands accordingly. This cycle will continue until the cost to the central bank of additional inflation just offsets the incentive to raise output. Output will be no different than if the central bank could precommit to zero inflation, but welfare will be lower because inflation is higher.

A zero-inflation rule is one conceivable response to the problems of the political business cycle and of time consistency, but a binding rule may be politically infeasible. In addition, it may be undesirable to limit the discretion of monetary policymakers so completely. Rules with clearly specified contingencies, or escape clauses, are preferable in theory (see Grossman and Van Huyck, 1988; Flood and Isard, 1989; Giovannini, 1993). In practice, however, the relevant contingencies are likely to be framed in terms of private information, in which case contingent rules lack credibility (Canzoneri, 1985) and discretion may be preferable.

Another alternative to binding rules, as Rogoff (1985) has shown, is the appointment of a conservative central banker who is more inflation adverse than is the public. This will bias policy toward lower inflation, which is welfare improving in the presence of time inconsistency.

A conservative central banker can only influence policy, of course, if he or she is independent of the government. Grilli, Masciandaro, and Tabellini (1991) construct measures of the political and economic independence of central banks. Political independence—the ability of a central bank to choose its policy objectives without constraints or influence from the government—is measured by three factors: whether or not the governor and the board are appointed by elected officials and for how long their appointments run; whether a government representative sits on the board and government approval of the board's decisions is required; and whether statute requires the central bank to pursue monetary stability or, alternatively, creates scope for conflict between the bank and government over issues like debt management. As shown in the top panel of Figure 6, the central banks of Germany and the Netherlands are the most politically independent of European central banks, and those of Belgium and the United Kingdom are the least. There is a significant negative correlation between political independence and the average annual inflation rate in the 1980s (shown on the vertical axis).

Grilli, Masciandaro, and Tabellini (1991) also construct measures of economic independence, or the freedom the central bank enjoys to use monetary-policy instruments to achieve monetary-policy goals. Their index is a function of limits placed on monetary financing of budget deficits and of constraints on the central bank's ability to discount commercial paper, purchase public debt, or extend loans. (All enter positively into the index of economic independence.) As shown in the bottom panel of Figure 6, the German Bundesbank is economically the most independent European central bank and the Banca d'Italia the least. Again, there is a negative correlation between economic independence and inflation.

This evidence, although impressive, has limitations. It is clear from Figure 6 that factors besides central-bank independence also influence inflation. Belgian inflation in the 1980s was consistently below the EC average, for example, despite the Belgian National Bank's lack of political independence. The R-squared from a regression of inflation on a constant term and both measures of central-bank independence is only two-thirds, confirming that these measures leave unexplained a nonnegligible portion of the variation in inflation rates.

Moreover, investigators disagree about the actual independence enjoyed by various central banks. Kennedy (1991) and Neumann and von Hagen (1992), for example, give more guarded assessments than do other authors of the political independence of the German Bundesbank.

FIGURE 6

CENTRAL-BANK INDEPENDENCE AND INFLATION

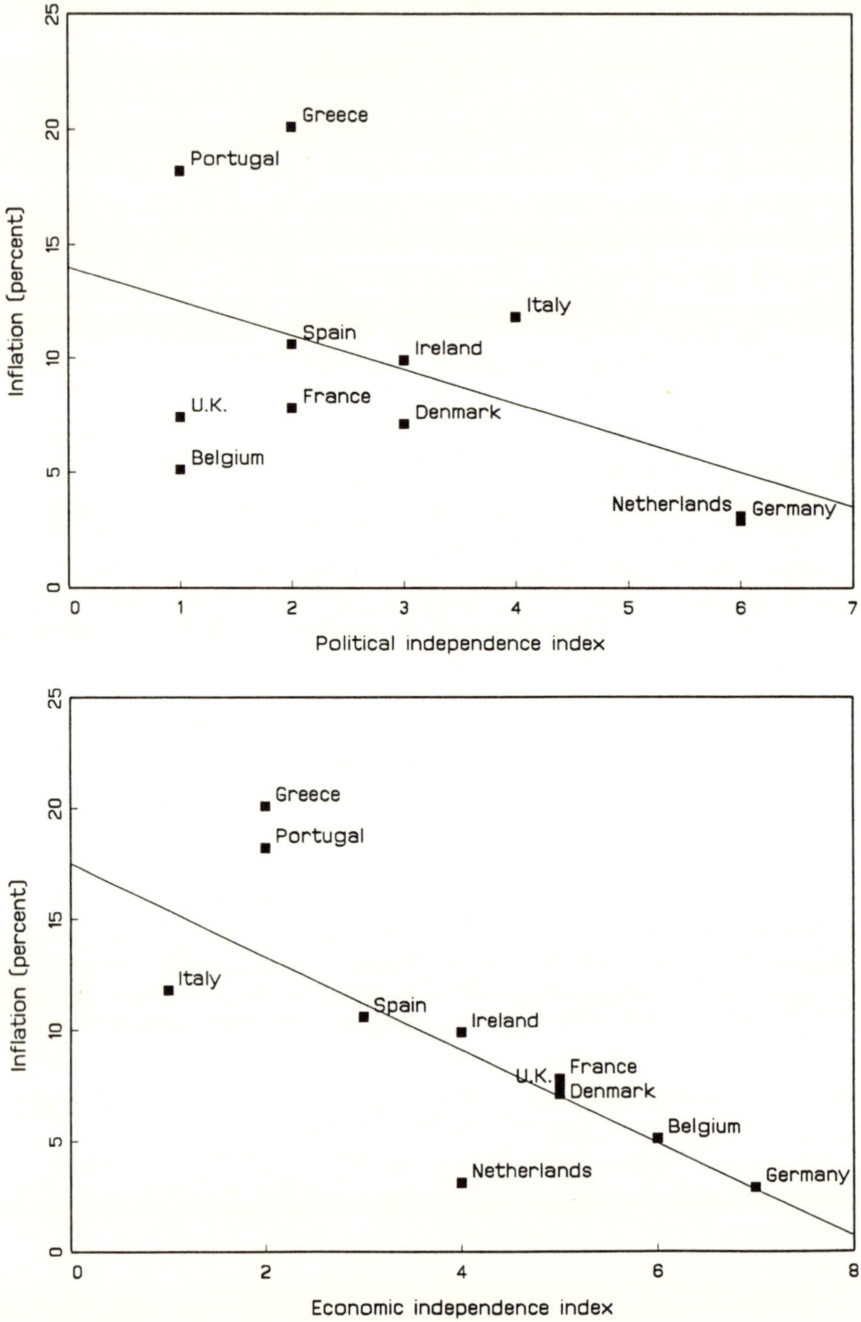

The events of September 1992, when Chancellor Helmut Kohl allegedly paid a secret visit to the Bundesbank to lobby for interest-rate reductions, underscore their skepticism.

Where would the ECB lie along these dimensions? Alesina and Grilli (1991) suggest that its statute positions it alongside the Bundesbank as the most independent of central banks. Its economic independence will be enhanced by a provision in its statute forbidding the ECB from providing lines of credit to EC or national public institutions. The statute prohibits representatives of the European Council from serving on the ECB's Governing Council, and Governing Council members are prohibited under the statute from receiving instructions from their national governments. Neither national governments nor other EC bodies must approve monetary-policy decisions.

Procedures for appointing the president and other members of the Executive Board are also consistent with high levels of political independence. The president's term of office will be eight years, as with the Bundesbank. The six members of the board (a subset of the Governing Council, comprised of the president, the vice president, and four additional members) will be chosen by the European Council for eight-year terms. The Governing Council itself will include both the Executive Board and the governors of the twelve national central banks. The statute specifies that they shall serve on the ECB's Governing Council for a minimum of five years. Executive Board members cannot be reappointed or dismissed for political reasons.

All of these conditions will buttress the independence of the ECB, enhancing its commitment to price stability. Nonetheless, questions can be raised about how independent and committed to price stability the new institution will be. Under Article 109b of the Maastricht Treaty, the president of the EC Council of Ministers and a member of the European Commission are permitted to participate in the Governing Council. Although not entitled to vote, the president of the Council of Ministers may submit a motion for deliberation. One can imagine that these representatives of political interests in the Community will thereby influence the deliberations of the Governing Council.

Moreover, national representatives will outnumber members at large on the Governing Council. This contrasts with the situation on the U.S. Federal Reserve System's Open Market Committee, where members at large constitute a majority. It has traditionally been true of this committee that officers of the regional reserve banks have been less activist than members of the board of governors (Puckett, 1984; Belden, 1989). Insofar as a common monetary policy is a blunt instrument for dealing with the problems of particular regions, one can imagine that national representatives will similarly be less inclined than members at large to push for an activist policy response. One can also imagine that, when regional conditions coincide, the dominance of national representatives could make it relatively easy to form a majority coalition of regional interests responsive to political pressures (say, countries with heavy debt burdens whose representatives would favor a more inflationary stance for monetary policy).

Finally, the Maastricht Treaty contains some complex provisions on the allocation of responsibility for monetary and exchange-rate policies. It empowers the Council of Ministers, and not the ECB, to conclude agreements on an exchange-rate system linking the ECU to non-EC currencies. Acting by a qualified majority, moreover, the Council of Ministers may change central rates for the ECU within such a system. Its decisions will bind the ECB, which will be compelled to implement them even if they clash with its other objectives. It is unclear what would happen if a Council of Ministers' decision regarding exchange-rate policy were to conflict with the ECB's mandate to insure price stability.

Responsibility for the Financial System

A striking feature of the Maastricht Treaty is the limited authority it gives the ECB to undertake financial surveillance and regulation. The ECB may undertake only such tasks of prudential supervision as are conferred on it by the European Council, which itself must act unanimously on a proposal from the European Commission and receive the assent of the European Parliament. These arrangements depart from those in monetary unions like the United States, where the central bank possesses extensive regulatory power.

There are three reasons why this divorce of monetary policy from prudential supervision may be undesirable. One is the danger that it will encourage competitive bank deregulation. European banks have traditionally enjoyed a favored position in their home markets. The 1992 Program will intensify international competition and allow intermediaries to better exploit economies of scale and scope (Chiappori et al., 1991, p. 70). Ultimately, some banks will be driven out of business, and national authorities will therefore be pressured to provide domestic banks with regulatory advantages. This situation will create externality problems insofar as the benefits from deregulation (in the form of profitability) accrue to bank shareholders and employees who are still primarily domestic, whereas the costs in the form of financial instability are incurred by the Community as a whole.

One potential form of competitive deregulation is the reduction or elimination of restrictions on the ratio of short-term bank assets to liabilities. In France, for example, assets with a maximum maturity of one month must be at least equal to liabilities of the same maximum maturity. In Germany, certain long-term assets must be matched with long-term liabilities, and medium-term assets must be matched with short- and medium-term liabilities. Relaxing these restrictions might heighten the illiquidity of European banks and weaken their ability to counter runs.

Competitive deregulation is a familiar problem. The 1988 Basle Accord, negotiated under the auspices of the Bank for International Settlements, was designed to prevent the competitive reduction of capital ratios by imposing uniform risk-weighted capital requirements. With minor modification, it provides the basis for the EC's Directives on Solvency Ratios and Own Funds, which are similarly intended to address the problem of competitive deregulation (Kapstein, 1991).

Even if capital requirements and liquidity ratios are standardized, the EC's Banking Directives still foresee enforcement at the national level. This leaves open the possibility that rules will be applied with varying degrees of stringency. Lax enforcement may therefore reintroduce all of the problems of different regulatory standards. Observers who take this problem seriously recommend centralizing surveillance and enforcement at the Community level.

A second problem with subsidiarity is that market integration will blur the borders between national banking systems. The greater the extent to which banks operate in several European countries, the less clear it will be which national authority is responsible for oversight. In an effort to insure a clear division of labor, the EC's Second Banking Directive states that credit institutions should be supervised by their home countries, whereas host countries should be responsible for liquidity standards. This home-country principle applies only to branches of foreign banks, however, and not to subsidiaries separately incorporated under the laws of host countries. Only greater centralization of regulatory functions is certain to eliminate confusion over the division of responsibilities.

A third problem with subsidiarity is that changes in the structure of European banking may heighten the need for a lender of last resort. As European banks branch out across national borders, they create new opportunities for banking panics to cross borders as well. Information costs will increase for depositors seeking to distinguish solvent from insolvent banks. "Life-boat operations," in which consortia of domestic banks aid their illiquid domestic counterparts, will become increasingly difficult to arrange as more of the relevant banks have their principal interests outside the country. All this may heighten the need for central-bank intervention and, correspondingly, supervision.

The securitization of financial assets and liabilities may also contribute to the need for a lender of last resort. European countries, aside from Great Britain and to a lesser extent France, have lagged behind the United States in the securitization of credit claims, ownership claims, and derivative contracts. Securitization, although solving one problem by enhancing the liquidity of banks' assets, creates another problem when traders and brokers in security markets find themselves exposed in the event of a crash. Folkerts-Landau and Garber (1991) argue that financial systems with liquid, securitized money and capital markets are even more likely than bank-intermediated financial systems to experience liquidity crises. Such systems have a greater need for a lender of last resort in the event of settlement failure.

Given the tendency for securitized credit to be substituted for bank credit as financial systems mature, securitization will continue to increase in Europe. This trend is already evident in Germany, where there has been a significant rise in the number of initial public-equity offerings by mid-sized industrial companies (Folkerts-Landau and Garber, 1991). Hence, there may be a growing need for the intervention of a lender of last resort even in countries like Germany, where it has traditionally been absent.

It is worth considering how bank regulation is reconciled with monetary union in highly securitized financial markets like that of the United States. A first implication of this comparison is that monetary union requires regulatory coordination but not total uniformity and centralization. The U.S. regulatory system is administered by both state and federal agencies, and responsibility at the federal level is divided between the central bank and other entities. For many years, capital requirements differed across jurisdictions. Smaller banks had to meet higher capital standards on the grounds that they held riskier, less diversified portfolios. (Uniform capital requirements were substituted in the 1980s because of improved access of small banks to secondary markets.) Enforcement of regulatory standards varies across jurisdictions: some regulators employ broad measures of capital, including long-term debt instruments such as subordinated notes and debentures, that others disavow.

Figure 7 summarizes the division of responsibilities among the various regulators. The Federal Reserve System possesses some regulatory authority over all banks, including noninsured state banks, to which it

FIGURE 7

THE TANGLED WEB OF BANK REGULATION

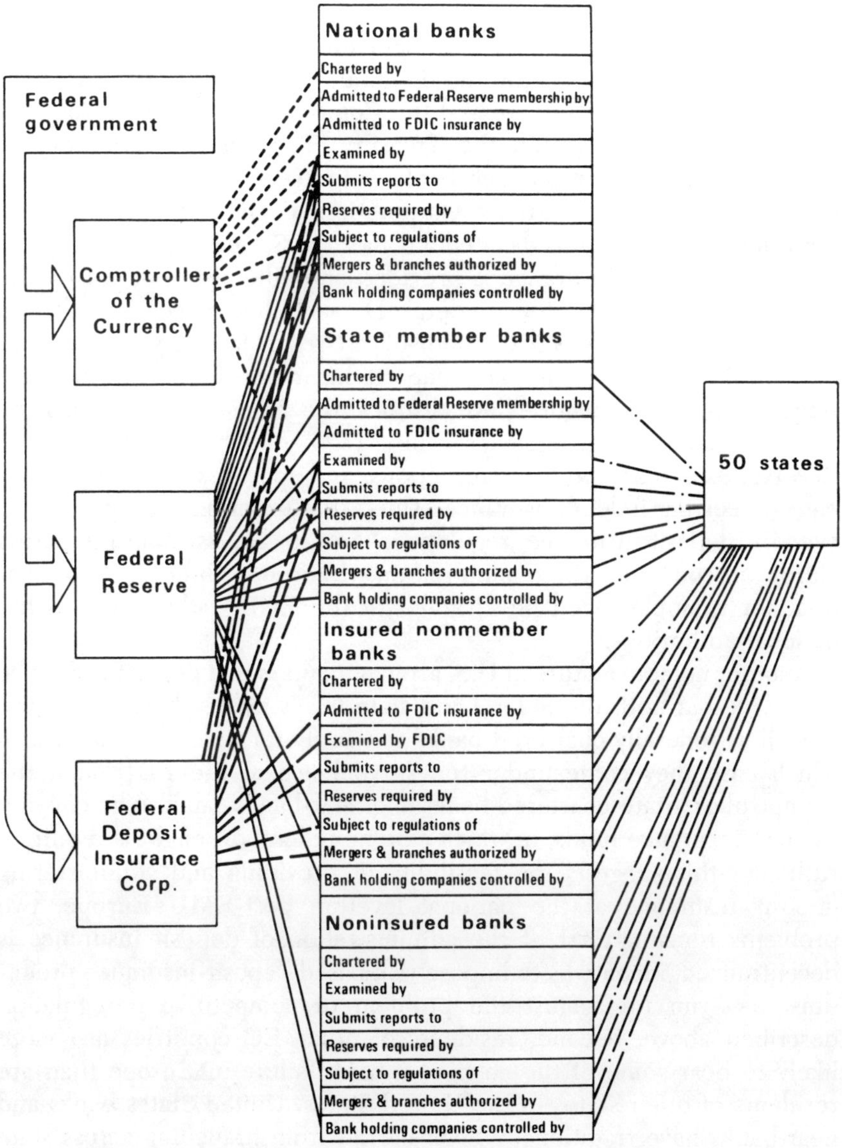

SOURCE: U.S. Congress, Senate Committee on Banking, Housing and Urban Affairs, Subcommittee on Financial Institutions, *Hearings on Financial Structure and Regulation*, 93rd Congress, 1st Session, 1973. p. 619.

may have to provide lender-of-last-resort facilities. But the Federal Reserve does not examine these banks, and the reports they must submit are limited. Thus, U.S. arrangements are consistent with the case for locating some but not all regulatory functions in the ECB.

Equally striking is the fact that regulatory responsibility for national banks that are members of the Federal Reserve System is divided between the Federal Reserve and the Comptroller of the Currency, an autonomous agency within the Treasury. The Comptroller, not the Federal Reserve, charters such banks, admits them to membership in the Federal Deposit Insurance Corporation (FDIC), and even screens them for membership in the Federal Reserve System.

Federal deposit insurance is provided and administered, not by the central bank, but by the Federal Deposit Insurance Corporation (FDIC). The rationale is that lender-of-last-resort facilities are designed for illiquid banks, closure and deposit insurance for insolvent ones. Because the two categories are distinct, the relevant services can be provided by different agencies. The FDIC, rather than the Federal Reserve, examines, requires corrections, and approves mergers of state banks receiving federal insurance. Thus, U.S. experience suggests that, even if deposit-insurance regulations are to be harmonized across European countries, there is no reason why responsibility for examination, for example, need be assigned to the ECB, rather than to the national authorities.

Another notable feature of U.S. arrangements is that deposit insurance is provided at both the federal and state levels. State-chartered banks, as well as federally chartered banks can apply for federal insurance, in which case they come under the surveillance of the FDIC and the Comptroller. State-chartered banks and near-banks can also be covered by state insurance funds, in which case no federal oversight is required. Although this suggests the feasibility of providing and administering deposit insurance at the national level in post-EMU Europe, two problems remain. First, if the administration of deposit insurance is decentralized, incentives to impose risk-based deposit-insurance premiums may run up against the problem of competitive deregulation described above. Second, residents of other EC countries are more likely to bear some of the costs of a bank failure in Europe than are residents of other states in the United States. United States banks and near-banks have traditionally been barred from branching across state lines. Few residents of other states were affected, for example, by the recent failure of cooperative savings banks in Rhode Island. Although this situation is changing, most banks involved in interstate operations are federally insured.

That Figure 7 is entitled "The Tangled Web of Bank Regulations" reflects the view that decentralization has gone too far in the United States. This degree of decentralization, to the extent that it is a legacy of history rather than a rational construct, might be an undesirable model for Europe. Prohibitions of interstate branching long justified the delegation of regulatory powers to state authorities. In the United States, as in Europe, this may have to change. In any case, there is no reason why regulatory authority in Europe must imitate the U.S. division into four distinct agencies.

In addition to being undesirable, a fire wall between monetary policy and prudential supervision may be unnecessary. The main argument against making the ECB responsible for the stability of the banking system—that this would create conflicts with the goal of price stability—is not supported by U.S experience. Lending of last resort occurs in response to major financial problems when other monetary assets are being liquidated. Hence, it need not have inflationary consequences. In 1929, the Federal Reserve Bank of New York provided liquidity to American financial markets in response to the Wall Street crash. In 1987, the Federal Reserve again provided extensive liquidity in the wake of a stock-market crash. In both cases, the additional liquidity was removed once the crisis had passed and had little impact on the money supply, much less on the price level. If lending of last resort is limited to exceptional crises, then it is hard to see why it should be any more of a threat to price stability in Europe than in the United States.

6 TRANSITIONAL ISSUES

The Rationale for Preconditions

If, during Stage II of the EMU process (to begin in 1994), the Council of Ministers decides that a majority of member countries meet the preconditions for monetary union, it may inaugurate Stage III, establishing the ECB and transferring to it responsibility for the conduct of monetary policy. This requires the assent of a qualified majority of national representatives at an extraordinary session of the Council attended by the heads of state or government. To prevent the indefinite continuation of Stage II, the Maastricht negotiators also specified a terminal date. The EC heads of state or government must meet no later than December 31, 1997 to assess whether a majority of EC member countries satisfy the entry conditions and to decide whether to set a date for the beginning of Stage III. If no date has been set by the end of 1997, Stage III will begin no later than January 1, 1999. In this latter case, EMU may go forward with the participation of only a minority of EC countries.

What preconditions must countries meet to enter Stage III? The treaty specifies four. First, countries must achieve a high degree of price stability, defined as an average rate of CPI inflation over the preceding twelve months that does not exceed the inflation rates of the three lowest-inflation member states by more than 1.5 percentage points. Second, they must have maintained stable exchange rates (within the normal EMS fluctuation bands) for the two preceding years without devaluing their currencies on their own initiative. Third, their long-term interest rates over the preceding year must have been no more than 2 percentage points above those of the three best performing member states in terms of inflation. Fourth, they must have achieved a "sustainable fiscal position," defined in a protocol to the treaty as a budget deficit no larger than 3 percent of GDP and a gross public debt no larger than 60 percent of GDP (subject to the qualifications and exceptions detailed at the end of the first section of Chapter 4 above).

The economic rationale for these fiscal criteria is not clear. Possibly they can be justified on the grounds that there exist two types of governments—those possessing and those lacking fiscal discipline—and that a smoothly functioning monetary union requires the exclusion of governments lacking discipline, the identity of which the Maastricht criteria are sufficient to recognize.

Canzoneri and Diba (1991) model a situation in which there exist two types of governments: one whose preference for government spending coincides with the public's, one that attaches more utility to government spending than does the public. Governments lacking fiscal discipline will, at the expense of public welfare, engage in a higher level of public spending financed by a higher level of distortionary taxation. (Discipline might be lacking when spending decisions are decentralized, when governments have short expected durations, when the constituency is highly polarized, and when governments engage in excessive spending prior to elections in order to maximize their reelection probability [see Corsetti and Roubini, 1992].) The central bank, even if it is interested in the utility of the public rather than that of the government, will increase the rate of money creation; it will maximize public welfare by solving the Ramsey-Phelps optimal-public-finance problem, balancing the costs of higher distortionary taxation against the deadweight loss from additional seigniorage. By printing more money and turning the proceeds over to the government, it will moderate the extent to which distortionary taxes have to rise.

Thus, whether or not the central bank is independent, it will not find it optimal to follow a zero-inflation policy, and claims to this effect will lack credibility. Even an independent central bank will fail to achieve price stability if the government lacks fiscal discipline.

If the independent central bank could credibly precommit to zero inflation, welfare would be enhanced. The deadweight loss associated with the reduction in real-money balances would be eliminated, and additional fiscal discipline would be imposed on the government, for the cost of financing its expenditure (through distortionary taxation alone) would have been raised. In these circumstances, the government's lack of fiscal discipline would be diminished rather than exacerbated by the establishment of a European central bank committed to price stability, and inadequate fiscal discipline has no implications for the efficiency of monetary policy.

The case for preconditions must rest, therefore, on the belief that a binding zero-inflation rule is impractical. Assume that rules are impractical for reasons such as those detailed in section one of Chapter 4 and that it is desirable to form a monetary union only of fiscally disciplined governments. Will the Maastricht criteria distinguish such governments from their undisciplined counterparts? Because undisciplined governments will be inclined to run budget deficits, fiscal criteria defined in terms of the deficit share of GNP are the obvious way of identifying them. There is no reason, however, why governments possessing fiscal discipline (with the same taste for government expenditure as the public) should be expected to keep their deficit spending below some arbitrary fraction of GDP. They will wish to run deficits in periods when the marginal utility of both public and private spending is relatively high. When the marginal utility of private spending is high, the marginal cost of taxation is also high, and governments wishing to maximize the welfare of domestic residents will run deficits and accumulate debt that will be serviced and/or repaid in subsequent periods when the marginal utility of public and private spending is low (Frenkel and Razin, 1987; Corsetti and Roubini, 1992). Welfare-maximizing governments will wish to smooth the marginal cost of taxation over time, running deficits in periods of large negative-output shocks.

Thus, if the marginal utility of spending rises dramatically (if, for example, incomes fall dramatically), it may be optimal even for a disciplined government to run deficits in excess of 3 percent of GNP. The Maastricht cutoff is entirely arbitrary. The same argument applies to the debt limit of 60 percent of GDP. This criterion is more appealing than the deficit threshold because it allows governments to run deficits in some periods and surpluses in others, as fiscally disciplined governments will wish to do when faced with random shocks to national income. It attempts to distinguish disciplined from undisciplined governments according to the magnitude and persistence of those deficits, as reflected in the level of public debt.[23] Once again, however, the 60-percent threshold selected at Maastricht is arbitrary. A fiscally disciplined government faced with a sequence of bad realizations of a stochastic income process might well run a series of deficits causing it to breach this threshold.

Even if all observers could agree on the appropriate levels at which to set these debt and deficit ratios, the resulting criteria might still fail to differentiate between governments possessing and lacking fiscal discipline. Backus and Driffill (1985) show that, when the public is imperfectly capable of distinguishing between disciplined and lax

[23] This is where the convergence criteria defined in terms of inflation and exchange-rate stability presumably come into play. If only public debt, and not fiscal deficit ratios, were to be used to determine whether a country qualified for participation in EMU, governments might attempt to inflate away the debt by depreciating the currency and raising the price level.

governments, a government lacking fiscal discipline may masquerade as its more disciplined counterpart.[24] It may emulate the policies followed by more disciplined governments, until a final period (in this context, the moment when it is irrevocably decided which countries qualify for inclusion in EMU), when it reveals its true type by pursuing undisciplined policies.

Under what conditions is this masquerade likely to occur? In the Backus-Driffill model, governments lacking discipline are most likely to continue emulating their more disciplined counterparts if they begin with a good reputation. Because the public will most probably believe that the government possesses fiscal discipline, it will not demand higher wages and higher interest rates on government debt (in anticipation of higher future public spending and inflation) until the government reveals its true type. The better the government's initial reputation, the longer the public will grant it these benefits, and the longer the government is likely to postpone revealing its type. Convergence criteria like those adopted at Maastricht are likely to be relatively efficient at ascertaining the true nature of a government currently possessing a questionable reputation, but they will be much less capable of providing useful information about a government whose current reputation is relatively good.

Thus, economic theory provides a justification for admitting to EMU only countries exhibiting adequate fiscal discipline. But the specific convergence criteria adopted at Maastricht are arbitrary and might well be violated by governments possessing the desired fiscal discipline. Furthermore, undisciplined counterparts, if they inherit favorable reputations, may succeed in masquerading as disciplined for an extended period. The Maastricht criteria may fail, therefore, to achieve their objectives.

From this same viewpoint, Corsetti and Roubini (1992) suggest revising Maastricht's fiscal conditions in two directions. First, escape clauses should be appended to the debt and deficit ceilings to permit governments to exceed them under well-defined contingencies. In the face of large negative shocks, larger deficits should be permitted. But the addition of (imperfectly observable) contingencies makes rules more difficult to enforce. To enhance the credibility of contingent rules, thereby preventing undisciplined governments from arbitrarily declaring

[24] The Backus-Driffill model is specified in terms of inflation and output rather than in terms of the links between public spending, on the one hand, and these variables, on the other, but this is of no consequence for the present analysis.

the existence of contingencies, it is important to strengthen the monitoring capacity and sanctions of the EC.

Timing the Transition

Leaving aside their desirability, what are the odds that the convergence criteria can be met by a majority of member countries? Table 8 shows the recent history of debts and deficits as percentages of GDP in member countries. These figures are approximate. They do not, for example, remove capital expenditures from government deficits, as the convergence criteria allow, but they still show that some countries have a long way to go. As of 1991, only three of the twelve members clearly met both fiscal criteria. The United Kingdom, hardly a steadfast proponent of monetary union, was one of the qualifiers (along with France and Luxembourg).

Certain other countries could qualify as well. Spain's public debt is below the Community average, and her budget deficit is within hailing distance of the Maastricht ceiling. Although Germany appears to violate the 3-percent deficit rule, reflecting the impact of GEMU on public expenditure, the large share of capital spending in the federal-government budget means that relatively small fiscal adjustments will allow Germany to meet this test. Although Denmark violates the 60-percent debt rule, three years of normal economic growth could bring that ratio below the Maastricht ceiling if the government succeeds in eliminating its budget deficit. Portugal's budget deficit is larger but her growth is faster; if the budget deficit is reduced to less than 3 percent of GDP, growth in excess of that rate would succeed in reducing the debt ratio to 60 percent.

Thus, seven member states might plausibly satisfy the Maastricht preconditions for monetary union by 1997. The Netherlands might also qualify if its budget deficit is eliminated and growth proceeds at 3 percent despite the contractionary fiscal shift. Other countries are in more difficult straits. Belgium's budget remains in substantial deficit, and normal economic growth can hardly halve a debt ratio of 130 percent by 1997. Not even a shift from 6-percent deficits to surpluses of the same magnitude would suffice. The Irish and Italian debts are 100 percent of GDP. Their budgets would have to swing from a 5- and 10-percent deficit, respectively, to substantial surplus, and to do so without interrupting economic growth, for the debt ratio to be reduced to 60 percent by the second half of the 1990s. Similarly, in Greece, with a debt ratio approaching 100 percent, normal economic growth cannot reduce the ratio to 60 percent in a mere five years; in addition, very

TABLE 8

MAIN INDICATORS OF NOMINAL CONVERGENCE PROBLEMS IN THE EC IN 1992

Country	Inflation		Public Finances			External Accounts		Interest Rates[a]	
	Deflator of Private Consumption	Nominal Unit Labor Costs	General Government Net Borrowing Requirement (% of GDP)	Public Debt as % of GDP: 1992	Public Debt as % of GDP: Change from 1991	Current-Account Balance (% of GDP)	National Savings (% of GDP)	Short Term	Long Term
Belgium	3.4	3.6	6.3	129.6	+0.2	1.1	21.1	9.5	9.2
Denmark	2.2	0.5	1.5	65.8	-0.9	2.2	19.8	9.1	10.0
Germany[b]	4.2	4.6	3.4	48.7	+2.5	-0.9	24.5	9.4	8.6
Greece	14.3	10.2	14.4	99.0	+2.6	-3.4	14.5	18.7	—
Spain	5.6	5.1	3.6	46.4	+0.8	-3.2	22.2	12.7	11.8
France	2.9	1.5	1.7	47.5	+0.3	-0.8	20.1	9.6	8.8
Ireland	3.0	3.9	4.1	100.4	-2.4	2.0	20.9	10.2	9.1
Italy	5.2	5.2	9.4	103.9	+2.7	-1.5	19.2	11.8	12.5
Luxembourg	3.7	2.6	(-2.0)	6.5	-0.4	26.1	54.8	—	—
Netherlands	3.5	3.5	4.1	79.5	+1.1	4.4	24.2	9.4	8.9
Portugal	9.5	12.5	4.6	62.7	-2.0	-1.5	26.4	17.7	16.6
United Kingdom	4.6	3.0	3.6	45.6	+1.8	-2.4	13.4	10.5	9.7
EC	4.5	3.9	4.3	63.3	+1.5	-0.5	20.2	10.7	10.1

SOURCE: Dixon, 1992, p. 6.

[a] Interest-rates are for November 1991; October 1991 for Greece.

[b] Public-finance and current-account figures are for the new German state.

substantial deficits would have to be replaced with surpluses in a way that does not interrupt growth even temporarily.

Thus, none of these countries is likely to meet the 60-percent debt requirement merely by eliminating its budget deficit and allowing normal economic growth to erode the ratio.[25] For them to gain admission, Maastricht's fiscal criteria (particularly the provision that a debt ratio may exceed 60 percent if it is "sufficiently diminishing . . . at a satisfactory pace") would have to be interpreted liberally.

Another option is to establish an EMU with seven members before 1999. Some observers, like Dornbusch (1990), have recommended a two-speed or two-track EMU, with the fast track to commence as soon as possible. The exchange-market crisis of September 1992, which pointed out the limitations of efforts to date to achieve monetary and fiscal convergence, seems to render an EMU comprised of a subset of EC members increasingly likely in the short run.

The efficiency gains from a single currency, however, are an increasing function of the number of countries that share it. If the benefits of EMU decline when fewer countries participate, why rush if it means limiting the number of participants? A two-speed EMU is justified only if the costs of EMU decline faster than its benefits as membership is limited.

Bayoumi and Eichengreen (1993c) have considered whether EC countries can be sorted into two groups according to the incidence and magnitude of disturbances and the speeds of adjustment to them. We identified two distinct groups of countries. In one, the EC "core" comprised of Germany, France, Belgium, Denmark, and the Netherlands, aggregate supply and demand disturbances were highly correlated across countries and speed of adjustment was relatively fast. In the other, the EC "periphery," shocks were larger and more idiosyncratic and adjustment was slower. (See Figures 4 and 5 above.) The core countries would incur a relatively low cost by forsaking the exchange-rate instrument and joining Germany in a monetary union at an early date.

Note, however, that the core countries singled out by this procedure as candidates for joining quickly are not those that would be identified by Maastricht's convergence criteria. The core-country group includes France, which already satisfies the Maastricht criteria, and Denmark and

[25] Corsetti and Roubini (1992) analyze the fiscal situation of these countries using solvency tests and arrive at essentially the same categorization as in the text.

the Netherlands, which conceivably might satisfy them, but it also includes Belgium, whose high debt ratio would bar early entry.

Furthermore, compared to these EC core members, shocks to the United Kingdom, Spanish, and Portuguese economies are larger and less well correlated with shocks to Germany. They will find the cost of forsaking exchange-rate changes against the deutsche mark to be relatively high. Yet, Maastricht's fiscal criteria identify them as candidates for early EMU membership. This, too, suggests that the fiscal provisions of the treaty are a suboptimal way of identifying potential participants.

One way of increasing the scope of the monetary union would be to admit more countries to the Community. Austria, Sweden, Norway, and Finland have debt ratios below 60 percent of GDP, and, except for Finland, their 1991 budget deficits were all less than 3 percent of GDP. All of these countries have expressed an interest in joining the Community. Expanding the EC to sixteen countries could thus produce a majority of members that satisfy the fiscal conditions at an early date. Admitting the other countries of the European Free Trade Association (EFTA), Switzerland and Iceland, would not tip the balance, because Switzerland satisfies the fiscal criteria although Iceland does not.

In any case, initiating a two-speed EMU in 1996 through the inclusion of these countries is not necessarily desirable on grounds of an optimum-currency area. Bayoumi and Eichengreen (1993a) analyze the incidence and magnitude of shocks to these economies, finding that Austria and Sweden belong with the EC core, whereas Norway and Finland more closely resemble the EC periphery. Once again, Maastricht's fiscal conditions do not seem to discriminate ideally among potential participants.

7 IMPACT ON THE REST OF THE WORLD

Compared to its impact on Europe, EMU's implications for the rest of the world have attracted less attention. (See, however, Alogoskoufis and Portes, 1991; Dornbusch 1991; Kenen 1992.) These implications can be considered under two headings: implications for international currencies and implications for international policy coordination.

Implications for the Demand for Currencies

A popular presumption is that creation of a single European currency will significantly increase the global demand for the ECU and reduce the demand for its competitors. In this chapter, I challenge this presumption. My argument is that, even if EMU stimulates the demand for ECUs and reduces the demand for dollars, the net effect is likely to be small, partly because historical and institutional factors inhibit shifts among currencies, partly because the desire for diversified portfolios should stimulate the demand for non-European currencies.

Money has three uses: as a store of value, a unit of account, and a medium of exchange. The ECU should be more attractive than existing European currencies on all three scores. If the ECB's commitment to price stability is honored, the ECU will be no less attractive as a store of value than the deutsche mark and more attractive than other European currencies. Residents of regions like Eastern Europe, who had previously acquired dollars as a store of value and a medium of exchange, will increasingly use ECUs instead. The ECU will be the unit of account for residents of the Community, who previously quoted prices and denominated contracts in one of the twelve national currencies. Insofar as creation of the Single Market stimulates European economic growth, the zone within which the ECU serves as unit of account will expand relative to other parts of the world. The ECU should emerge as an increasingly attractive medium of exchange for residents of other countries who trade with this rapidly expanding European market. For all these reasons, one result of EMU may be an ECU that gains importance relative to the dollar and even the yen.

At the same time, it is important not to overlook the fact that the desirability of an asset as a unit of account and a medium of exchange in international transactions is partly a function of how many other traders use it as such (Matsuyama, Kiyotaki, and Matsui, 1991). This network externality tends to lock in international currencies long after the disappearance of the historical circumstances that led to their emergence. The British pound, for example, retained disproportionate importance as an international currency long after World War II, although Britain had lost her status as the world's predominant commercial and financial power. The same can now be said of the dollar, in which 45 percent of industrial-country imports and exports were invoiced as recently as 1987 (when the U.S. share of their commodity exports was only half that large). Currently, about one-fifth of the EC's trade is invoiced in dollars.[26] So long as traders continue to use dollars as a medium of exchange, each individual trader will hesitate to switch to the ECU. The ECU may gradually acquire greater importance relative to the dollar as a medium of exchange in extra-European transactions. The European Commission (1990) conjectures that perhaps half of the one-fifth of European trade currently invoiced in dollars will eventually be invoiced in ECUs, thereby increasing by $60 billion the demand for ECUs for transactions purposes. This amount will be larger still if the countries of Eastern Europe adopt the ECU as their international currency. The tendency for network externalities and economies of scale to lock in existing international currencies will, however, slow the transition.

The aspect of the problem that is most difficult to forecast is the demand for ECU-denominated financial assets as investments. In 1988, fully half of global private-sector wealth denominated in foreign currencies was held in dollars, with only a quarter in EC currencies, although the two economies accounted for comparable shares of global GNP. Such demands depend on the risk-and-return characteristics of the competing assets. There is no obvious reason to think that the real rate of return on ECU-denominated assets will be significantly different than the real returns on, say, deutsche marks. It is true that financial liberalization and increased competition among European intermediaries may reduce the spread between bank-deposit and loan rates and reduce bid-ask spreads on other financial assets, thereby raising the returns to private investors. Any such change, however, will be small.

Trends in the demand for European financial assets will hinge, rather, on the ECU's risk characteristics relative to existing currencies. Most discussion of this question proceeds on the assumption that the ECB will honor its commitment to price stability, thereby eliminating one

[26] Insofar as they represent mainly trade in oil, however, figures such as these may overstate the economic significance of invoicing in dollars.

traditional source of risk. If the ECB achieves this goal, the asset demand for ECUs will be stimulated, raising their share in private portfolios by as much as 5 percentage points, according to European Commission estimates. But investor behavior is influenced not merely by the risk of unforeseen changes in returns, but also by the covariance of those changes across assets. Investors hold diversified portfolios to limit risk. Hence, the demand for ECU-denominated assets may fall relative to the demand for assets denominated in existing national currencies, insofar as investors are no longer able to diversify away risk by holding portfolios containing several different European currencies. Traditionally, when the dollar has been strong, the deutsche mark has been weak relative to other European currencies, and, when the dollar has been weak, the deutsche mark has been strong in the EMS (Frankel, 1986). From the vantage point of a French investor with the bulk of her portfolio in francs, this tendency creates an incentive to hold both dollars and deutsche marks in order to diversify away some risk. Following EMU, investors in countries like France will have most of their wealth denominated in units of the single European currency. To minimize the risks caused by its fluctuation, they may find it attractive to hold additional dollars. Contrary to the conventional wisdom, the demand for the major non-European currencies may thereby be stimulated by EMU.

Implications for Policy Coordination

Will EMU make the coordination of macroeconomic policies easier or harder to achieve? Replacing twelve European central banks with the ECB will reduce the number of players in the international policy game, which might appear to diminish the free-rider problem that complicates efforts to arrange pareto-improving policy trades. Substituting the ECB for the Bank of England, the Bank of France, the Bank of Italy, and the Bundesbank might seem sufficient to effectively transform the Group of 7 (G-7) into a Group of 4 (G-4) when the leading industrial-country monetary policymakers meet.

Unfortunately, the key actors in G-7 meetings are finance ministers, not central bankers. The central banks are not even represented at the deputy level. The tradition of allowing finance ministers to speak for Europe's monetary as well as fiscal authorities will become increasingly problematic as central-bank independence is buttressed in Stages II and III of the EMU process. There will be one EC central bank, but there will continue to be twelve finance ministers, and Article 109 of the Maastricht Treaty does not detail the nature of cooperation between them. While emphasizing the need for the Community to speak with a single voice, it does not specify who should do the talking. Will the finance minister of the country occupying the EC presidency represent the Community in G-7 summits? Will the independent president of the ECB also have a voice?

It is particularly unclear who will represent the EC in discussions of exchange-rate management.[27] The Council of Ministers is responsible for exchange-rate agreements with the rest of the world, the ECB is responsible for monetary management. Are exchange-rate-policy initiatives undertaken in concert with the United States, Canada, and Japan an instance of the former or the latter, and what role in their formulation and execution will be taken by the Council of Ministers, national finance ministries, and officials of the ECB? Who, for example, would have represented the Community at the Plaza or the Louvre?

Matters will be complicated further under the increasingly plausible assumption that EMU will proceed at two speeds. The subset of EC members participating initially will be represented on the ECB's Governing Council, but not the others, possibly including Britain and Italy, both of which belong to the G-7. In response to this problem, the treaty makes provision for another decision-making body, the General Council, which is comprised of the president and vice president of the ECB and all twelve EC central-bank governors, irrespective of whether their countries currently participate in EMU. The General Council of the twelve, rather than the Governing Council of the seven, could conceivably speak for Europe's central banks in negotiations with the United States, Canada, and Japan. But the General Council will possess little real decision-making power. It may "contribute" to the work of the ECB through the collection of statistical information and the oversight of personnel matters, but its authority will not clearly extend to monetary policies, domestic or international. It is not guaranteed the right to be informed on matters pending before the Governing Council; it will only be notified of decisions taken by it.

In any case, major questions related to the EC's efforts to coordinate policies with the rest of the world may be decided, not by the Governing Council, but by the Council of Ministers. Although all twelve EC

[27] Kenen (1992, pp. 119-120) points out that, although the relevant portions of the Maastricht Treaty are opaque, passages such as "the Council shall . . . decide," "the Council may . . . formulate," and "the Council may . . . adopt, adjust or abandon," appear to create a presumption that the Council will be the Community's representative, acting in consultation with the ECB.

countries are represented on the Council of Ministers, those not yet participating in EMU may not be able to vote on matters covered by Article 109. They will then demand their own separate representation. Suppose that the United Kingdom opts out of EMU; will the G-7 then effectively become a G-4½ comprised of the United States, Canada, Japan, the EC, and the United Kingdom?

In addition to blurring lines of authority, the transition to Stage III creates other complications for policy coordination. If the ECB is anxious to signal the priority it attaches to price stability, it may hesitate to engage in a simultaneous adjustment of monetary policies with the United States and Japan if that adjustment entails loosening European monetary policy. If European governments are prevented from running budget deficits larger than 3 percent of GDP, the scope for coordinating fiscal policies with the United States and Japan may be restricted.

These problems are solvable. Once the ECB's commitment to price stability is established, it can exercise discretion without damaging its reputation. The Maastricht Treaty allows the fiscal thresholds to be interpreted flexibly, which will become easier to do once the ECB has established its unwillingness to bail out fiscally insolvent governments.

The question, as noted by Alogoskoufis and Portes (1991), then becomes how monetary unification will affect cooperation in practice. In Eichengreen (1992b), I identify three fundamental obstacles to international policy coordination: domestic political constraints, international political disputes, and incompatible analytical frameworks. Frankel (1988) has emphasized the importance of the last factor. It is only by the sheerest coincidence, he shows, that policymakers in different countries will be able to agree on a concerted response to their common economic problems if they cannot agree on a diagnosis. The popularity of the EMU process itself reflects a convergence of economic thinking in Europe, and the continual interaction of national officials on the ECB's Governing Council should serve to solidify this common analytical outlook. Whether this common model will converge to or diverge from the models that prevail in other countries is more difficult to say. To the extent that the European model comes to resemble that of Germany, it will tend to diverge from that of the United States. The German authorities, in contrast to the dominant strand of thinking in the United States, deny that monetary expansion can effectively stimulate economic activity and argue that fiscal expansion tends to weaken the exchange rate and the balance of payments.

Domestic political constraints have repeatedly interfered with governments' efforts to arrange mutually beneficial adjustments in policies with their foreign counterparts (Putnam, 1988). The problem has been evident in the General Agreement on Tariffs and Trade (GATT) negotiations, in which the European agricultural lobby has resisted reductions in agricultural protection. The same problem exists in the realm of monetary policy; debtors, for example, tend to benefit from lower interest rates, creditors from higher ones. Insofar as Stage II requires that the independence of existing central banks be strengthened, and insofar as the ECB will enjoy even greater insulation from domestic political pressures than national central banks enjoy, domestic political constraints on policy coordination may become less binding.

Finally, international disputes over matters other than macroeconomic policy may sour the climate of good will that facilitates macroeconomic policy coordination. Trade conflicts between Europe and the United States, for example, would discourage the harmonization of trans-Atlantic monetary policies. The prospect that the transition to EMU will give rise to adjustment problems characterized by pockets of high unemployment, in response to which Europe may be tempted to limit competition from abroad by putting up its common external tariff or erecting other external trade barriers, does not bode well, therefore, for international macroeconomic policy coordination.

8 POLICY IMPLICATIONS

The scholarly literature sounds important warnings about possible adverse implications of EMU for Europe and the rest of the world. It does not follow, however, that the goal of European monetary union is undesirable or the process fatally flawed. Indeed, the potential gains are considerable. The goal for European policymakers in the wake of the Danish and French referenda should be to reduce the costs in order to insure that they are dominated by the benefits.

The costs can be minimized by modifying the Maastricht Treaty. It should be refined to allocate more clearly responsibility for exchange-rate policy and to facilitate policy coordination at G-7 summits. Provisions that inhibit the ECB from undertaking prudential supervision should be relaxed. Similarly, although one can debate how important a role fiscal federalism has played in existing monetary unions, it is hard to dispute that a more extensive system of regional coinsurance would help to absorb asymmetric shocks. Along similar lines, although the EC has already begun to mandate the portability of pensions and Community-wide recognition of technical qualifications, more such steps are needed to enhance labor mobility and to facilitate adjustment through migration.

Such measures will be politically contentious, because they are at odds with the principle of subsidiarity. Creating a Community-wide system of fiscal federalism capable of providing regional coinsurance on a significant scale would require not only reshaping existing programs like the Structural Funds, but also transferring existing fiscal functions of member states to the Community. Endowing the ECB with responsibility for prudential supervision will similarly limit the autonomy of national regulatory authorities. Measures to enhance labor mobility will diminish the scope for member states to structure and regulate their national labor markets.

One popular interpretation of the Danish and French referenda is that the Single Market Program is seen as a threat to national autonomy. This judgment creates an incentive for EC officials to reemphasize the principal of subsidiarity as a political expedient for pushing their program through. The message in this study is that doing so may ultimately create larger problems that threaten the viability of EMU.

REFERENCES

A'Hearn, Brian, "Migration and Economic Convergence in Post-War Italy," University of California at Berkeley, 1991, processed.

Advisory Commission on Intergovernmental Relations (ACIR), *Fiscal Discipline in the Federal System: National Reform and the Experience of the States*, Washington, D.C., Advisory Commission on Intergovernmental Relations, 1987.

Alesina, Alberto, "Politics and Business Cycles in Industrial Democracies," *Economic Policy*, 8 (April 1989), pp. 55-98.

Alesina, Alberto, and Vittorio Grilli, "The European Central Bank: Reshaping Monetary Politics in Europe," CEPR Discussion Paper No. 563, London, Centre for Economic Policy Research, July 1991.

Allen, Steven, "Changes in the Cyclical Sensitivity of Wages in the United States: 1891-1987," *The American Economic Review*, 82 (No. 1, March 1992), pp. 122-140.

Alogoskoufis, George, and Richard Portes, "International Costs and Benefits from EMU," *European Economy*, Special Issue No. 1, 1991, pp. 231-245.

Alt, James B., and Robert C. Lowry, "Divided Government and Budget Deficits: Evidence from the States," Harvard University, 1992, processed.

Attanasio, Orazio P., and Fiorella Padoa Schioppa, "Regional Inequalities, Migration and Mismatch in Italy, 1960-86," in Fiorella Padoa Schioppa, ed., *Mismatch and Labour Mobility*, Cambridge and New York, Cambridge University Press, 1991, pp. 237-321.

Backus, David, and John Driffill, "Inflation and Reputation," *The American Economic Review*, 75 (No. 3, June 1985), pp. 530-538.

Baldwin, Richard, "The Growth Effects of 1992," *Economic Policy*, 9 (October 1989), pp. 248-281.

Barro, Robert and David Gordon, "Rules, Discretion and Reputation in a Model of Monetary Policy," *Journal of Monetary Economics*, 12 (No. 1, July 1983), pp. 101-121.

Bayoumi, Tamim, "A Note on the Decomposition of Vector Autoregressions," *International Monetary Fund Staff Papers*, 39 (No. 2, June 1992), pp. 330-356.

Bayoumi, Tamim, and Barry Eichengreen, "Is There a Conflict Between EC Enlargement and European Monetary Unification?" *Greek Economic Review*, forthcoming 1993a.

———, "Monetary and Exchange Rate Arrangements for NAFTA," *Journal of Development Economics*, forthcoming 1993b.

———, "Shocking Aspects of European Monetary Unification," in Francesco Giavazzi and Francisco Torres, eds., *The Transition to Economic and Monetary Union in Europe*, Cambridge and New York, Cambridge University Press, forthcoming 1993c.

Bayoumi, Tamim, Morris Goldstein, and Geoffrey Woglom, "State and Local Government Finances in the Current Cycle," International Monetary Fund, 1992, processed.

Bayoumi, Tamim, and James Gordon, "The Determinants and Efficiency of Local Authority Spending in England," International Monetary Fund, 1991, processed.

Bayoumi, Tamim, and Paul Masson, "Fiscal Flows in the United States and Canada: Lessons for Monetary Union in Europe," International Monetary Fund, 1991, processed.

Belden, Susan, "Policy Preferences of POMC Members as Revealed by Dissenting Votes," *Journal of Money, Credit, and Banking*, 21 (No. 4, November 1989), pp. 432-441.

Bini-Smaghi, Lorenzo, and Silvia Vori, "Rating the EC as an Optimum Currency Area: Is it Worse than the U.S.?" Banca d'Italia, 1992, processed.

Blanchard, Olivier, and Lawrence Katz, "Regional Evolutions," *Brookings Papers on Economic Activity*, 1 (1992), pp. 1-61.

Blanchard, Olivier, and Danny Quah, "The Dynamic Effects of Aggregate Demand and Supply Disturbances," *The American Economic Review*, 79 (No. 4, September 1989), pp. 655-673.

Bruno, Michael, and Jeffrey Sachs, *The Economics of Worldwide Stagflation*, Cambridge, Mass., Harvard University Press, 1985.

Canzoneri, Matthew, "Monetary Policy Games and the Role of Private Information," *The American Economic Review*, 75 (No. 5, December 1985), pp. 1056-1070.

Canzoneri, Matthew, and Behzad Diba, "Fiscal Deficits, Financial Integration, and a Central Bank for Europe," *Journal of the Japanese and International Economies*, 5 (No. 4, December 1991), pp. 381-403.

Chiappori, Pierre-André, Colin Mayer, Damien Neven, and Xavier Vives, "The Microeconomics of Monetary Union," in Centre for Economic Policy Research, *Monitoring European Integration: The Making of Monetary Union*, London, Centre for Economic Policy Research, 1991, pp. 69-120.

Collins, Susan, "Inflation and the European Monetary System," in Francesco Giavazzi, Stefano Micossi, and Marcus Miller, eds., *The European Monetary System: Proceedings of a Conference Organised by the Banca d'Italia, STEP, and CEPR*, Cambridge and New York, Cambridge University Press, 1988, pp. 112-136.

Collins, Susan, and Francesco Giavazzi, "Attitudes Toward Inflation and the Viability of Fixed Exchange Rates: Evidence from the EMS," in Michael Bordo and Barry Eichengreen, eds., *A Retrospective on the Bretton Woods System: Lessons for International Monetary Reform*, Chicago, University of Chicago Press, forthcoming 1993.

Commission of the European Communities, *Report of the Study Group on the Role of Public Finance in European Integration* [MacDougall Report], Brussels, Commission of the European Communities, 1977.

———, "One Market, One Money," *European Economy*, No. 44, October 1990.

Committee for the Study of Economic and Monetary Union [Delors Report], *Report on Economic and Monetary Union in the European Community*, Luxembourg, Office for Official Publications of the European Communities, 1989.

Conference of the Representatives of the Governments of the Member States, *Amendments to the EEC Treaty—Economic and Monetary Union—As Agreed in the European Council of Maastricht on 10 December 1991*, 1991, processed draft.

Corsetti, Giancarlo, and Nouriel Roubini, "Tax Smoothing Discretion versus Balanced Budget Rules in the Presence of Politically Motivated Fiscal Deficits: The Design of Optimal Fiscal Rules for Europe After 1992," CEPR Discussion Paper No. 682, London, Centre for Economic Policy Research, August 1992.

Cushman, David, "Exchange-Rate Uncertainty and Foreign Direct Investment in the United States," *Weltwirtschaftliches Archiv*, 124 (No. 2, 1988), pp. 322-336.

De Grauwe, Paul, *The Economics of Monetary Integration*, Oxford, Oxford University Press, 1992.

De Grauwe, Paul, and Wim Vanhaverbeke, "Is Europe an Optimum Currency Area? Evidence from Regional Data," CEPR Discussion Paper No. 555, London, Centre for Economic Policy Research, May 1991.

Dixon, Joly, "The Maastricht Conclusions on Economic and Monetary Union," Commission of the European Communities, 1992, processed.

Dornbusch, Rudiger, "Two-Track EMU, Now!" in Karl Otto Pöhl, Richard Layard, and Rudiger Dornbusch, eds., *Britain and EMU*, London, Centre for Economic Performance in association with Financial Markets Group, London School of Economics, 1990, pp. 103-111.

———, "Europe's Money: Implications for the Dollar," testimony before the Subcommittee on Domestic Monetary Policy, U.S. House of Representatives, July 25, 1991.

Dowd, Kevin, "Does Europe Need a Federal Reserve System?" *The Cato Journal*, 2 (Fall 1990), pp. 423-442.

Doyle, Maurice F., "Regional Policy and European Economic Integration," in Committee for the Study of Economic and Monetary Union, *Report on Economic and Monetary Union in the European Community*, Luxembourg, Office of Official Publications of the European Communities, 1989, pp. 69-79.

Eichengreen, Barry, "The U.S. Capital Market and Foreign Lending, 1920-1955," in Jeffrey Sachs, ed., *Developing Country Debt and Economic Performance, Volume I: The International Financial System*, Chicago, University of Chicago Press, 1989, pp. 107-158.

———, "One Money for Europe? Lessons from the U.S. Currency and Customs Union," *Economic Policy*, 10 (April 1990), pp. 117-187.

———, "Designing a Central Bank for Europe: A Cautionary Tale from the Early Years of the Federal Reserve System," in Matthew Canzoneri, Vittorio Grilli, and Paul Masson, eds., *Designing a European Central Bank*,

Cambridge and New York, Cambridge University Press, 1992a, pp. 13-40.

———, *Golden Fetters: The Gold Standard and the Great Depression, 1919-1939*, New York, Oxford University Press, 1992b.

———, "Is Europe an Optimum Currency Area?," CEPR Discussion Paper No. 478, in Silvio Borner and Herbert Grubel, eds., *The European Community After 1992: The View From Outside*, London, Macmillan, 1992c.

———, "Labor Markets and European Monetary Unification," in Paul Masson and Mark Taylor, eds., *Policy Issues in the Operation of Currency Unions*, Cambridge and New York, Cambridge University Press, forthcoming 1993a.

———, "The Political Economy of Fiscal Policy Under EMU," *Stato e Mercato*, forthcoming 1993b.

Emerson, Michael, "The Economics of 1992: An Assessment of the Potential Economic Effects of Completing the Internal Market of the European Economy," *European Economy*, No. 35, March 1988.

Fleming, J. Marcus, "Domestic Financial Policies Under Fixed and Under Flexible Exchange Rates," *International Monetary Fund Staff Papers*, 9 (No. 3, November 1962), pp. 369-380.

Flood, Robert, and Peter Isard, "Monetary Policy Strategies," *International Monetary Fund Staff Papers*, 36 (No. 3, September 1989), pp. 612-632.

Flood, Robert, Andrew Rose, and Donald Mathieson, "The Empirical Exploration of Exchange Rate Target Zones," Carnegie-Rochester Conference Series on Public Policy 35 (Autumn 1991), pp. 7-66.

Folkerts-Landau, David, and Peter M. Garber, "The ECB: A Bank or a Monetary Policy Rule?" Mario Monti and Richard Portes, eds., *The Road to EMU*, London, Centre for Economic Policy Research, 1991.

Frankel, Jeffrey A., "The Implications of Mean-Variance Optimization for Four Questions in International Macroeconomics," *Journal of International Money and Finance*, 5, supplement (March 1986), pp. 53-75.

———, *Obstacles to International Macroeconomic Policy Coordination*, Princeton Studies in International Finance No. 64, Princeton, N.J., Princeton University, International Finance Section, December 1988.

Frankel, Jeffrey A., and Steven Phillips, "The European Monetary System: Credible at Last?" National Bureau of Economic Research Working Paper No. 3819, Cambridge, Mass., National Bureau of Economic Research, August 1991.

Fratianni, Michele, Jürgen von Hagen, and Christopher Waller, "From EMS to EMU," Indiana University, 1991, processed.

———, *The Maastricht Way to EMU*, Essays in International Finance No. 187, Princeton, N.J., Princeton University, International Finance Section, June 1992.

Frenkel, Jacob A., and Assaf Razin, *Fiscal Policies in the World Economy*, Cambridge, Mass., MIT Press, 1987.

Froot, Kenneth, and Kenneth Rogoff, "The EMS, the EMU, and the Transition to a Common Currency," *NBER Macroeconomics Annual*, 6 (1991), pp. 269-317.

Gerlach, Stefan, "Adjustable Pegs vs. Single Currencies: How Valuable is the Option to Realign?" Brandeis University, 1991, processed.

Giavazzi, Francesco, and Marco Pagano, "Confidence Crises and Public Debt Management," in Rudiger Dornbusch and Mario Draghi, eds., *Public Debt Management: Theory and History*, Cambridge and New York, Cambridge University Press, 1990, pp. 125-142.

Giovannini, Alberto, "The Currency Reform as the Last Stage of Economic and Monetary Union, Some Policy Questions," CEPR Discussion Paper No. 591, London, Centre for Economic Policy Research, October 1991.

———, "Desirable EMU," *The Economist*, July 11-17, 1992, p. 6.

———, "Bretton Woods and its Precursors: Rules Versus Discretion in the History of International Monetary Regimes," in Michael Bordo and Barry Eichengreen, eds., *A Retrospective on the Bretton Woods System: Lessons for International Monetary Reform*, Chicago, University of Chicago Press, forthcoming 1993.

Glick, Reuven, and Michael Hutchinson, "Fiscal Policy in Monetary Unions: Implications for Europe," *Open Economy Review*, 4 (November 1992), pp. 39-65.

Goldstein, Morris, and Geoffrey Woglom, "Market-Based Fiscal Discipline in Monetary Unions: Evidence from the U.S. Municipal Bond Market," in Matthew Canzoneri, Vittorio Grilli, and Paul Masson, eds., *Establishing a Central Bank: Issues in Europe and Lessons from the US*, Cambridge and New York, Cambridge University Press, 1992, pp. 228-270.

Gordon, James, "Structural Funds and the 1992 Program in the European Community," International Monetary Fund, 1991, processed.

Grilli, Vittorio, Donato Masciandaro, and Guido Tabellini, "Political and Monetary Institutions and Public Financial Policies in the Industrial Countries," *Economic Policy*, 13 (October 1991), pp. 341-392.

Gros, Daniel, and Niels Thygesen, *European Monetary Integration: From the European Monetary System to European Monetary Union*, London, Longmans, 1992.

Grossman, Herschel I., and John B. Van Huyck, "Sovereign Debt as a Contingent Claim: Excusable Default, Repudiation, and Reputation," *The American Economic Review*, 78 (No. 5, December 1988), pp. 1088-1097.

Ingram, James C., "State and Regional Payments Mechanisms," *The Quarterly Journal of Economics*, 73 (November 1959), pp. 619-632.

International Monetary Fund (IMF), "Exchange Rate Volatility and World Trade," processed, 1983.

Kapstein, Ethan B., *Supervising International Banks: Origins and Implications of the Basle Accord*, Essays in International Finance No. 185, Princeton, N.J., Princeton University, International Finance Section, December 1991.

Kenen, Peter B., "The Theory of Optimum Currency Areas: An Eclectic View," in Robert Mundell and Alexander Swoboda, eds., *Monetary Problems of the International Economy*, Chicago and London, University of Chicago Press, 1969, pp. 41-60.

———, "Exchange-Rate Variability: Measurement and Implications," Princeton University, 1979, processed.
———, *EMU After Maastricht*, Washington, D.C., Group of Thirty, 1992.
Kennedy, Ellen, *The Bundesbank: Germany's Central Bank in the International Monetary System*, London, Royal Institute of International Affairs, 1991.
Kiyotaki, Nobuhiro, and Randall Wright, "On Money as Medium of Exchange," *The Journal of Political Economy*, 97 (No. 4, August 1989), pp. 827-954.
Krugman, Paul, *Geography and Trade*, Leuven, Leuven University Press, and Cambridge, Mass., MIT Press, 1991.
———, "Integration, Specialization and Regional Growth: Notes on 1992, EMU and Stabilization," in Francesco Giavazzi and Francisco Torres, eds., *The Transition to Economic and Monetary Union in Europe*, Cambridge and New York, Cambridge University Press, forthcoming 1993.
Kydland, Finn, and Edward Prescott, "Rules Rather Than Discretion: The Inconsistency of Optimal Plans," *The Journal of Political Economy*, 85 (No. 3, June 1977), pp. 473-492.
McKinnon, Ronald, "Optimum Currency Areas," *The American Economic Review*, 53 (No. 4, September 1963), pp. 717-725.
———, "The Rules of the Game," *Journal of Economic Literature*, forthcoming 1993.
McLeod, Darryl, and John H. Welch, "The Case for a Peso Target Zone," *Business Mexico*, 1 (November 1991a), pp. 19-22.
———, "Free Trade and the Peso," Fordham University and Federal Reserve Bank of Dallas, 1991b, processed.
Masson, Paul, and Jacques Melitz, "Fiscal Policy Independence in a European Monetary Union," *Open Economies Review*, 2 (No. 2, 1991), pp. 113-136.
Masson, Paul, and Mark P. Taylor, "Common Currency Areas and Currency Unions: An Analysis of the Issues," International Monetary Fund, 1991, processed.
Matsuyama, Kiminori, Nobuhiro Kiyotaki, and Akihiko Matsui, "Toward a Theory of International Currency," Northwestern University, London School of Economics, and University of Pennsylvania, 1991, processed.
Morsink, R., and Willem Molle, "Direct Investment and Monetary Integration," *European Economy*, Special Issue No. 1, 1991, pp. 36-55.
Mundell, Robert, "A Theory of Optimum Currency Areas," *The American Economic Review*, 51 (No. 4, September 1961), pp. 657-665.
———, "Capital Mobility and Stabilization Policy Under Fixed and Flexible Exchange Rates," *The Canadian Journal of Economics* 29 (November 1963), pp. 475-485.
Neumann, Manfred J., "Central Bank Independence as a Prerequisite of Price Stability," *European Economy*, Special Issue No. 1, 1991, pp. 79-92.
———, "Exchange Rate Mechanism Remains Valid Alternative to Single European Currency," *Financial Times* (London), July 11, 1992.
Neumann, Manfred J., and Jürgen von Hagen, "Monetary Policy in Germany," in Michele Fratianni and Dominick Salvatore, eds., *Monetary Policy in*

Developed Economies (*Handbook of Comparative Economic Policies*, Vol. 3), New York, Greenwood Press, forthcoming 1993.

Obstfeld, Maurice, "Destabilizing Effects of Exchange Rate Escape Clauses," in Mario Monti and Richard Portes, eds., *The Road to EMU*, London, Centre for Economic Policy Research, 1992.

Organisation for Economic Co-operation and Development (OECD), *Flexibility in the Labor Market*, Paris, Organisation for Economic Co-operation and Development, 1986.

——, *Substructural Adjustment in OECD Countries*, Paris, Organisation for Economic Co-operation and Development, 1989.

Pissarides, Christopher, and Ian McMaster, "Regional Migration, Wage and Unemployment: Empirical Evidence and Implications for Policy," *Oxford Economic Papers*, 42 (No. 4, October 1990), pp. 812-831.

Puckett, Richard S., "Federal Open Market Committee Structure and Decisions," *Journal of Monetary Economics*, 14 (July 1984), pp. 97-104.

Putnam, Robert, "Diplomacy and Domestic Politics: The Logic of Two-Level Games," *International Organization*, 42 (No. 3, Summer 1988), pp. 427-460.

Rogoff, Kenneth, "The Optimal Degree of Commitment to an Intermediate Monetary Target," *The Quarterly Journal of Economics*, 100 (No. 4, November 1985), pp. 1168-1189.

Roubini, Nouriel, "Leadership and Cooperation in the European Monetary Union: A Simulation Approach," National Bureau of Economic Research Working Paper No. 3044, Cambridge, Mass., National Bureau of Economic Research, July 1989.

Russo, Massimo, and Giuseppe Tullio, "Monetary Policy Coordination within the EMS: Is There a Rule?" in Francesco Giavazzi, Stefano Micossi, and Marcus Miller, eds., *The European Monetary System: Proceedings of a Conference Organised by the Banca d'Italia, STEP, and CEPR*, Cambridge and New York, Cambridge University Press, 1988, pp. 292-356.

Sachs, Jeffrey, and Xavier Sala-i-Martin, "Federal Fiscal Policy and Optimum Currency Area," Harvard University, 1990, processed.

Sapir, André, and Khalid Sekkat, "Exchange Rate Variability and International Trade: The Effects of the European Monetary System," Free University of Brussels, 1989, processed.

Ungerer, Horst, Owen Evans, and Peter Nyberg, *The European Monetary System: Recent Developments*, Occasional Paper No. 48, Washington, D.C., International Monetary Fund, 1986.

U.S. Congress, Senate Committee on Banking, Housing and Urban Affairs, Subcommittee on Financial Institutions, *Hearings on Financial Structure and Regulation*, 93rd Congress, 1st Session, 1973.

van der Ploeg, Frederick, "Fiscal Aspects of Monetary Integration in Europe," CEPR Discussion Paper No. 340, London, Centre for Economic Policy Research, August 1989.

van Rompuy, Paul, Filip Abraham, and Dirk Heremans, "Economic Federalism and the EMU," *European Economy*, Special Issue No. 1, 1991, pp. 109-135.

von Hagen, Jürgen, "A Note on the Empirical Effectiveness of Formal Fiscal Restraints," *Journal of Public Economics*, 44 (No. 2, March 1990), pp. 199-210.

———, "Fiscal Arrangements in a Monetary Union: Evidence from the U.S.," Indiana University, 1991, processed.

Williamson, John, "Britain's Role in EMU," Institute for International Economics, 1990, processed.

Wright, Gavin, *Old South, New South: Revolutions in the Southern Economy Since the Civil War*, New York, Basic Books, 1986.

PUBLICATIONS OF THE
INTERNATIONAL FINANCE SECTION

Notice to Contributors

The International Finance Section publishes papers in four series: ESSAYS IN INTERNATIONAL FINANCE, PRINCETON STUDIES IN INTERNATIONAL FINANCE, and SPECIAL PAPERS IN INTERNATIONAL ECONOMICS contain new work not published elsewhere. REPRINTS IN INTERNATIONAL FINANCE reproduce journal articles previously published by Princeton faculty members associated with the Section. The Section welcomes the submission of manuscripts for publication under the following guidelines:

ESSAYS are meant to disseminate new views about international financial matters and should be accessible to well-informed nonspecialists as well as to professional economists. Technical terms, tables, and charts should be used sparingly; mathematics should be avoided.

STUDIES are devoted to new research on international finance, with preference given to empirical work. They should be comparable in originality and technical proficiency to papers published in leading economic journals. They should be of medium length, longer than a journal article but shorter than a book.

SPECIAL PAPERS are surveys of research on particular topics and should be suitable for use in undergraduate courses. They may be concerned with international trade as well as international finance. They should also be of medium length.

Manuscripts should be submitted in triplicate, typed single sided and double spaced throughout on 8½ by 11 white bond paper. Publication can be expedited if manuscripts are computer keyboarded in WordPerfect 5.1 or a compatible program. Additional instructions and a style guide are available from the Section.

How to Obtain Publications

The Section's publications are distributed free of charge to college, university, and public libraries and to nongovernmental, nonprofit research institutions. Eligible institutions may ask to be placed on the Section's permanent mailing list.

Individuals and institutions not qualifying for free distribution may receive all publications for the calendar year for a subscription fee of $35.00. Late subscribers will receive all back issues for the year during which they subscribe. Subscribers should notify the Section promptly of any change in address, giving the old address as well as the new.

Publications may be ordered individually, with payment made in advance. ESSAYS and REPRINTS cost $6.50 each; STUDIES and SPECIAL PAPERS cost $9.00. An additional $1.25 should be sent for postage and handling within the United States, Canada, and Mexico; $1.50 should be added for surface delivery outside the region.

All payments must be made in U.S. dollars. Subscription fees and charges for single issues will be waived for organizations and individuals in countries where foreign-exchange regulations prohibit dollar payments.

Please address all correspondence, submissions, and orders to:

International Finance Section
Department of Economics, Fisher Hall
Princeton University
Princeton, New Jersey 08544-1021

List of Recent Publications

A complete list of publications may be obtained from the International Finance Section.

ESSAYS IN INTERNATIONAL FINANCE

156. Sebastian Edwards, *The Order of Liberalization of the External Sector in Developing Countries*. (December 1984)
157. Wilfred J. Ethier and Richard C. Marston, eds., with Kindleberger, Guttentag and Herring, Wallich, Henderson, and Hinshaw, *International Financial Markets and Capital Movements: A Symposium in Honor of Arthur I. Bloomfield*. (September 1985)
158. Charles E. Dumas, *The Effects of Government Deficits: A Comparative Analysis of Crowding Out*. (October 1985)
159. Jeffrey A. Frankel, *Six Possible Meanings of "Overvaluation": The 1981-85 Dollar*. (December 1985)
160. Stanley W. Black, *Learning from Adversity: Policy Responses to Two Oil Shocks*. (December 1985)
161. Alexis Rieffel, *The Role of the Paris Club in Managing Debt Problems*. (December 1985)
162. Stephen E. Haynes, Michael M. Hutchison, and Raymond F. Mikesell, *Japanese Financial Policies and the U.S. Trade Deficit*. (April 1986)
163. Arminio Fraga, *German Reparations and Brazilian Debt: A Comparative Study*. (July 1986)
164. Jack M. Guttentag and Richard J. Herring, *Disaster Myopia in International Banking*. (September 1986)
165. Rudiger Dornbusch, *Inflation, Exchange Rates, and Stabilization*. (October 1986)
166. John Spraos, *IMF Conditionality: Ineffectual, Inefficient, Mistargeted*. (December 1986)
167. Rainer Stefano Masera, *An Increasing Role for the ECU: A Character in Search of a Script*. (June 1987)
168. Paul Mosley, *Conditionality as Bargaining Process: Structural-Adjustment Lending, 1980-86*. (October 1987)
169. Paul Volcker, Ralph Bryant, Leonhard Gleske, Gottfried Haberler, Alexandre Lamfalussy, Shijuro Ogata, Jesús Silva-Herzog, Ross Starr, James Tobin, and Robert Triffin, *International Monetary Cooperation: Essays in Honor of Henry C. Wallich*. (December 1987)
170. Shafiqul Islam, *The Dollar and the Policy-Performance-Confidence Mix*. (July 1988)
171. James M. Boughton, *The Monetary Approach to Exchange Rates: What Now Remains?* (October 1988)
172. Jack M. Guttentag and Richard M. Herring, *Accounting for Losses On Sovereign Debt: Implications for New Lending*. (May 1989)
173. Benjamin J. Cohen, *Developing-Country Debt: A Middle Way*. (May 1989)
174. Jeffrey D. Sachs, *New Approaches to the Latin American Debt Crisis*. (July 1989)

175. C. David Finch, *The IMF: The Record and the Prospect.* (September 1989)
176. Graham Bird, *Loan-loss Provisions and Third-World Debt.* (November 1989)
177. Ronald Findlay, *The "Triangular Trade" and the Atlantic Economy of the Eighteenth Century: A Simple General-Equilibrium Model.* (March 1990)
178. Alberto Giovannini, *The Transition to European Monetary Union.* (November 1990)
179. Michael L. Mussa, *Exchange Rates in Theory and in Reality.* (December 1990)
180. Warren L. Coats, Jr., Reinhard W. Furstenberg, and Peter Isard, *The SDR System and the Issue of Resource Transfers.* (December 1990)
181. George S. Tavlas, *On the International Use of Currencies: The Case of the Deutsche Mark.* (March 1991)
182. Tommaso Padoa-Schioppa, ed., with Michael Emerson, Kumiharu Shigehara, and Richard Portes, *Europe after 1992: Three Essays.* (May 1991)
183. Michael Bruno, *High Inflation and the Nominal Anchors of an Open Economy.* (June 1991)
184. Jacques J. Polak, *The Changing Nature of IMF Conditionality.* (September 1991)
185. Ethan B. Kapstein, *Supervising International Banks: Origins and Implications of the Basle Accord.* (December 1991)
186. Alessandro Giustiniani, Francesco Papadia, and Daniela Porciani, *Growth and Catch-Up in Central and Eastern Europe: Macroeconomic Effects on Western Countries.* (April 1992)
187. Michele Fratianni, Jürgen von Hagen, and Christopher Waller, *The Maastricht Way to EMU.* (June 1992)
188. Pierre-Richard Agénor, *Parallel Currency Markets in Developing Countries: Theory, Evidence, and Policy Implications.* (November 1992)

PRINCETON STUDIES IN INTERNATIONAL FINANCE

55. Marsha R. Shelburn, *Rules for Regulating Intervention under a Managed Float.* (December 1984)
56. Paul De Grauwe, Marc Janssens and Hilde Leliaert, *Real-Exchange-Rate Variability from 1920 to 1926 and 1973 to 1982.* (September 1985)
57. Stephen S. Golub, *The Current-Account Balance and the Dollar: 1977-78 and 1983-84.* (October 1986)
58. John T. Cuddington, *Capital Flight: Estimates, Issues, and Explanations.* (December 1986)
59. Vincent P. Crawford, *International Lending, Long-Term Credit Relationships, and Dynamic Contract Theory.* (March 1987)
60. Thorvaldur Gylfason, *Credit Policy and Economic Activity in Developing Countries with IMF Stabilization Programs.* (August 1987)
61. Stephen A. Schuker, *American "Reparations" to Germany, 1919-33: Implications for the Third-World Debt Crisis.* (July 1988)
62. Steven B. Kamin, *Devaluation, External Balance, and Macroeconomic Performance: A Look at the Numbers.* (August 1988)
63. Jacob A. Frenkel and Assaf Razin, *Spending, Taxes, and Deficits: International-Intertemporal Approach.* (December 1988)

64. Jeffrey A. Frankel, *Obstacles to International Macroeconomic Policy Coordination*. (December 1988)
65. Peter Hooper and Catherine L. Mann, *The Emergence and Persistence of the U.S. External Imbalance, 1980-87*. (October 1989)
66. Helmut Reisen, *Public Debt, External Competitiveness, and Fiscal Discipline in Developing Countries*. (November 1989)
67. Victor Argy, Warwick McKibbin, and Eric Siegloff, *Exchange-Rate Regimes for a Small Economy in a Multi-Country World*. (December 1989)
68. Mark Gersovitz and Christina H. Paxson, *The Economies of Africa and the Prices of Their Exports*. (October 1990)
69. Felipe Larraín and Andrés Velasco, *Can Swaps Solve the Debt Crisis? Lessons from the Chilean Experience*. (November 1990)
70. Kaushik Basu, *The International Debt Problem, Credit Rationing and Loan Pushing: Theory and Experience*. (October 1991)
71. Daniel Gros and Alfred Steinherr, *Economic Reform in the Soviet Union: Pas de Deux between Disintegration and Macroeconomic Destabilization*. (November 1991)
72. George M. von Furstenberg and Joseph P. Daniels, *Economic Summit Declarations, 1975-1989: Examining the Written Record of International Cooperation*. (February 1992)
73. Ishac Diwan and Dani Rodrik, *External Debt, Adjustment, and Burden Sharing: A Unified Framework*. (November 1992)
74. Barry Eichengreen, *Should the Maastricht Treaty Be Saved?*. (December 1992)

SPECIAL PAPERS IN INTERNATIONAL ECONOMICS

15. Gene M. Grossman and J. David Richardson, *Strategic Trade Policy: A Survey of Issues and Early Analysis*. (April 1985)
16. Elhanan Helpman, *Monopolistic Competition in Trade Theory*. (June 1990)
17. Richard Pomfret, *International Trade Policy with Imperfect Competition*. (August 1992)

REPRINTS IN INTERNATIONAL FINANCE

25. Jorge Braga de Macedo, *Trade and Financial Interdependence under Flexible Exchange Rates: The Pacific Area*; reprinted from *Pacific Growth and Financial Interdependence*, 1986. (June 1986)
26. Peter B. Kenen, *The Use of IMF Credit*; reprinted from *Pulling Together: The International Monetary Fund in a Multipolar World*, 1989. (December 1989)
27. Peter B. Kenen, *Transitional Arrangements for Trade and Payments Among the CMEA Countries*; reprinted from *International Monetary Fund Staff Papers* 38 (2), 1991. (July 1991)